Parasyte 4

HITOSHI IWAAKI

TRANSLATED AND ADAPTED BY ANDREW CUNNINGHAM
LETTERED BY FOLTZ DESIGN

BALLANTINE BOOKS • NEW YORK

Parasyte volume 4 is a work of fiction. Names, characters, places, and incidents are the products of the author's imagination or are used fictitiously. Any resemblance to actual events, locales, or persons, living or dead, is entirely coincidental.

A Del Rey Manga/Kodansha Trade Paperback Original

Published in the United States by Del Rey Books, an imprint of The Random House Publishing Group, a division of Random House, Inc., New York.

Del Rey is a registered trademark and the Del Rey colophon is a trademark of Random House, Inc.

Publication rights arranged through Kodansha Ltd.

First published in Japan in 2003 by Kodansha Ltd., Tokyo

ISBN 978-0-345-49826-7

Printed in the United States of America

www.delreymanga.com

9 8 7 6 5 4 3 2 1

Translator/adapter: Andrew Cunningham
Lettering: Foltz Design

CONTENTS

HONORIFICS EXPLAINED

Throughout the Del Rey Manga books, you will find Japanese honorifics left intact in the translations. For those not familiar with how the Japanese use honorifics and, more important, how they differ from American honorifics, we present this brief overview.

Politeness has always been a critical facet of Japanese culture. Ever since the feudal era, when Japan was a highly stratified society, use of honorifics—which can be defined as polite speech that indicates relationship or status—has played an essential role in the Japanese language. When addressing someone in Japanese, an honorific usually takes the form of a suffix attached to one's name (example: "Asuna-san"), is used as a title at the end of one's name, or appears in place of the name itself (example: "Negi-sensei," or simply "Sensei!").

Honorifics can be expressions of respect or endearment. In the context of manga and anime, honorifics give insight into the nature of the relationship between characters. Many English translations leave out these important honorifics and therefore distort the feel of the original Japanese. Because Japanese honorifics contain nuances that English honorifics lack, it is our policy at Del Rey not to translate them. Here, instead, is a guide to some of the honorifics you may encounter in Del Rey Manga.

-san: This is the most common honorific and is equivalent to Mr., Miss, Ms., or Mrs. It is the all-purpose honorific and can be used in any situation where politeness is required.

-sama: This is one level higher than "-san" and is used to confer great respect.

-dono: This comes from the word "tono," which means "lord." It is an even higher level than "-sama" and confers utmost respect.

-kun: This suffix is used at the end of boys' names to express familiarity or endearment. It is also sometimes used by men among friends, or when addressing someone younger or of a lower station.

-chan: This is used to express endearment, mostly toward girls. It is also used for little boys, pets, and even among lovers. It gives a sense of childish cuteness.

Bozu: This is an informal way to refer to a boy, similar to the English terms "kid" and "squirt."

Sempai/ Senpai: This title suggests that the addressee is one's senior in a group or organization. It is most often used in a school setting, where underclassmen refer to their upperclassmen as "sempai." It can also be used in the workplace, such as when a newer employee addresses an employee who has seniority in the company.

Kohai: This is the opposite of "sempai" and is used toward underclassmen in school or newcomers in the workplace. It connotes that the addressee is of a lower station.

Sensei: Literally meaning "one who has come before," this title is used for teachers, doctors, or masters of any profession or art.

-[blank]: This is usually forgotten in these lists, but it is perhaps the most significant difference between Japanese and English. The lack of honorific means that the speaker has permission to address the person in a very intimate way. Usually, only family, spouses, or very close friends have this kind of permission. Known as *yobisute*, it can be gratifying when someone who has earned the intimacy starts to call one by one's name without an honorific. But when that intimacy hasn't been earned, it can be very insulting.

HITOSHI IWAAKI

CONTENTS

CHAPTER 26: A GIRL'S DREAM

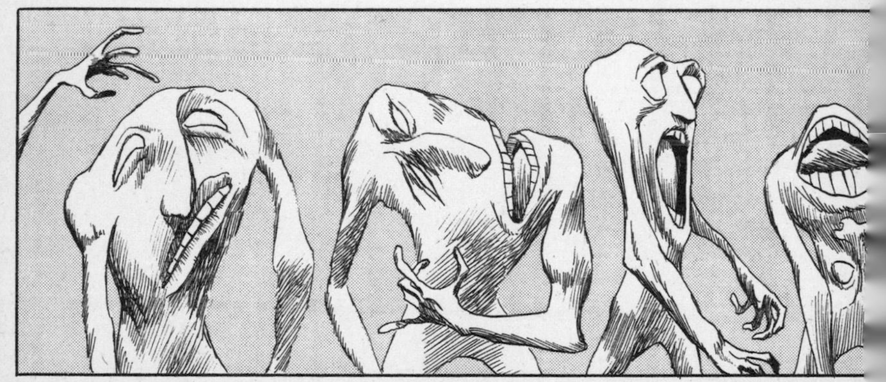

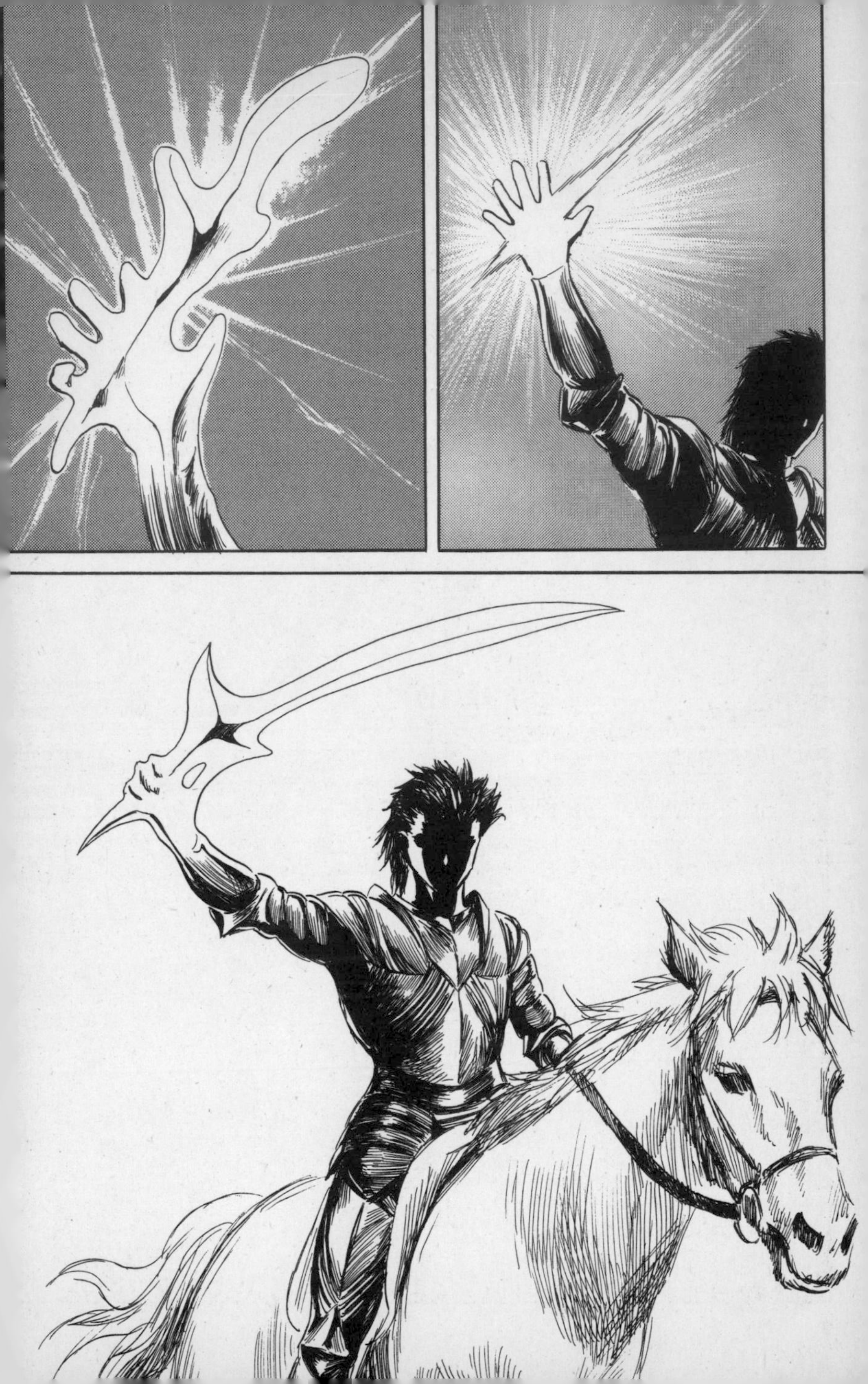

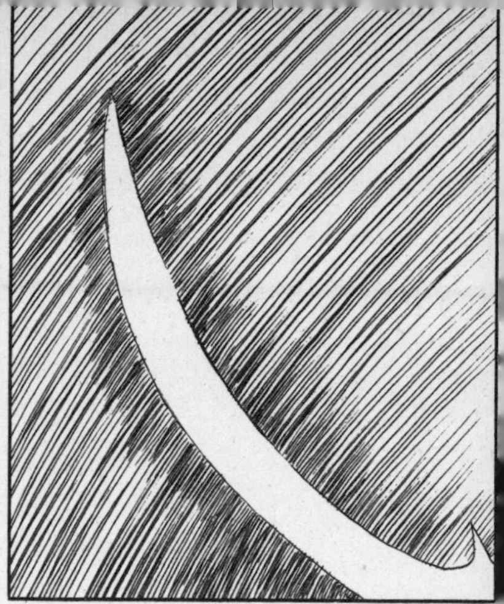

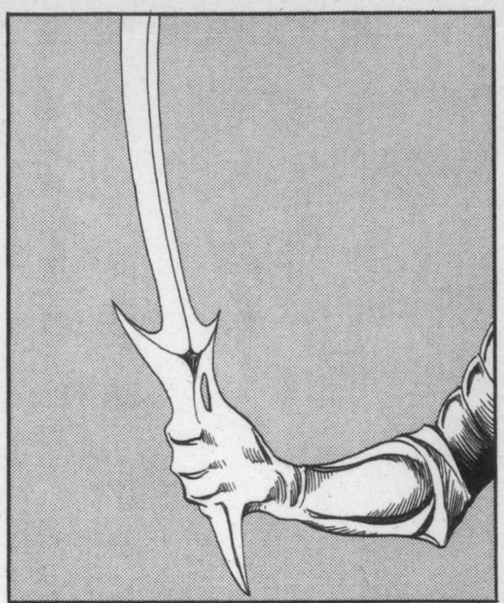
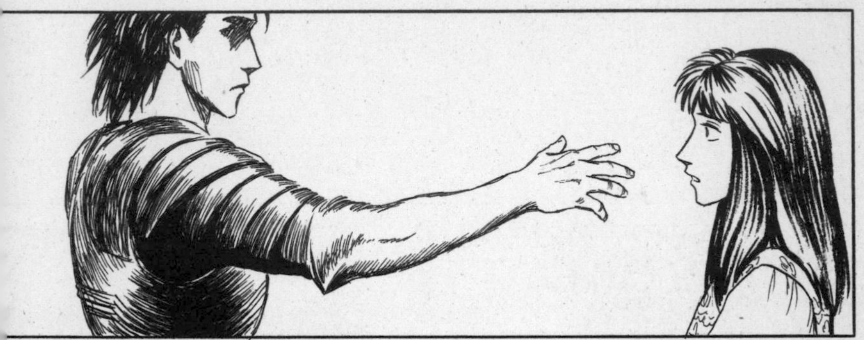

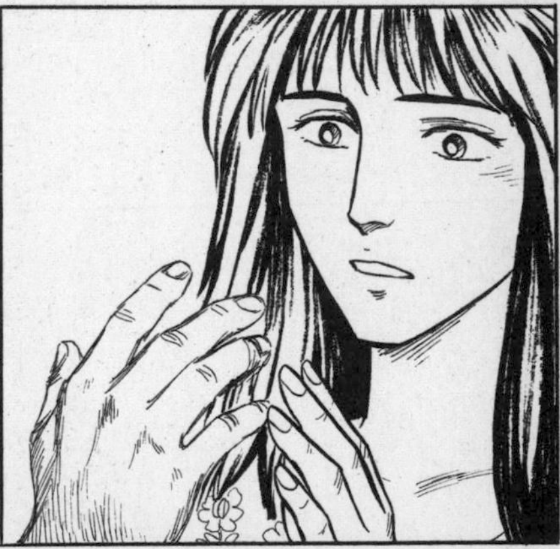

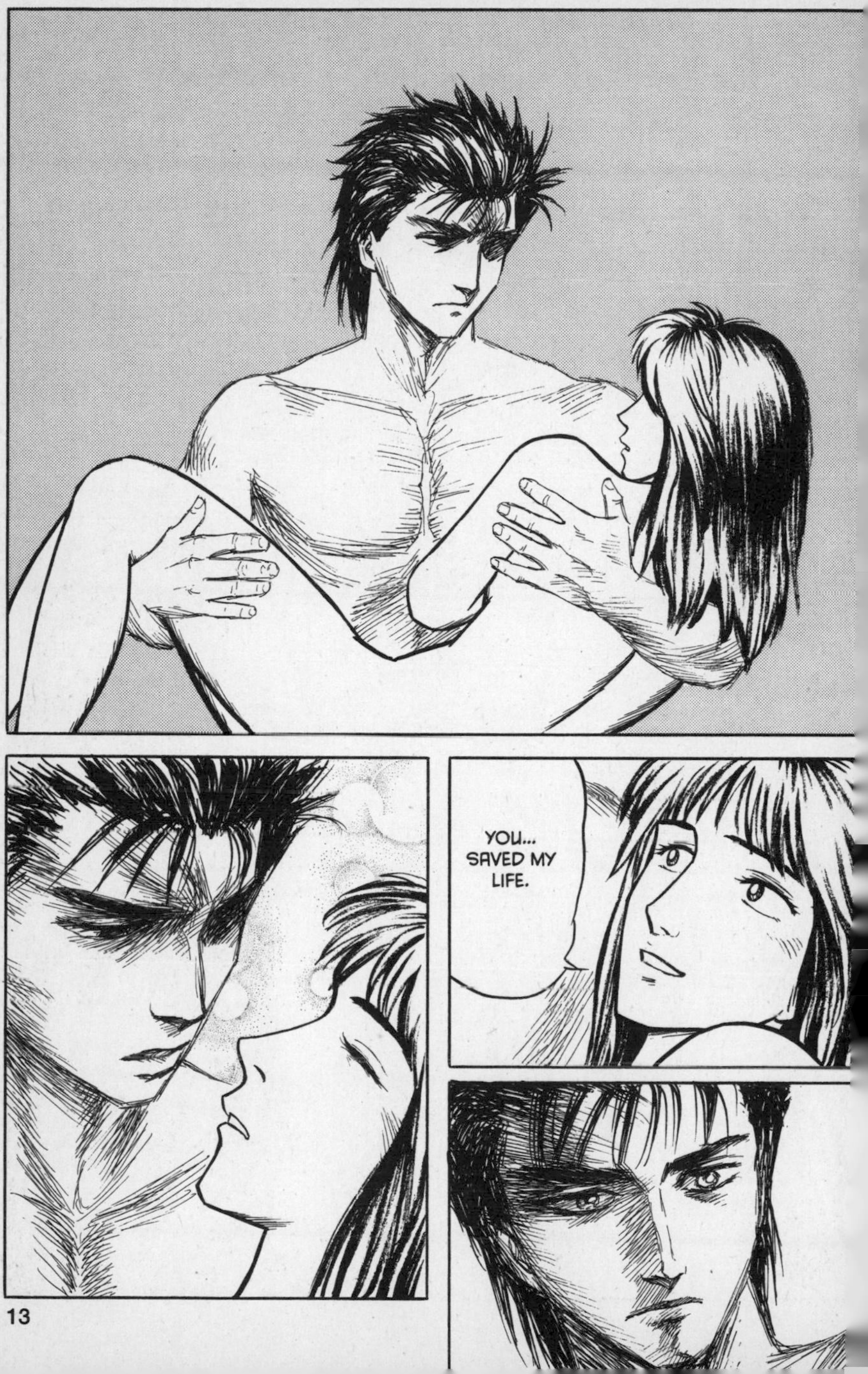

YOU...
SAVED MY
LIFE.

......

PFFT...

HA HA HA HA HA!
HEE HEE HEE HEE HA HA HA HA HA HA HA!

AH HA... AH HA...
HAHHH...

I'D RATHER DIE...
...THAN TELL ANYONE ABOUT *THAT* DREAM.

ARGH! THIS BLOWS.

KA-CHUNK
ゴトッ
KA-CHUNK
ゴトッ
......

WAS HE REALLY...
...RIDING A WHITE HORSE?

BWA HA HA HA!

HoLiDAY

KA-CHUNK
KA-CHUNK

SHA
PHOTOG
BY A STU
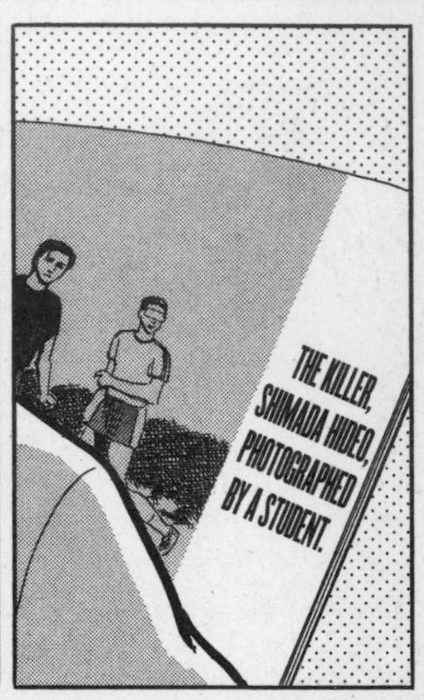
THE KILLER, SHIMADA HIDEO, PHOTOGRAPHED BY A STUDENT.

EH!? BUT THAT'S...

THAT'S STRANGE. IN WHAT WAY DO I LOOK LIKE IZUMI?

HEY! LET GO!

MON-STERS...

OKAY, LOOK. YOU CAN FEEL SOME-THING.
SOMETHING THAT DAN-GEROUS PEOPLE LIKE THAT GUY HAVE. LIKE AN AURA OR SOMETHING.

SO YOU'RE DANGEROUS, TOO?

Y-YEAH. I AM.

NO...WAY...

THAT AFTER-NOON
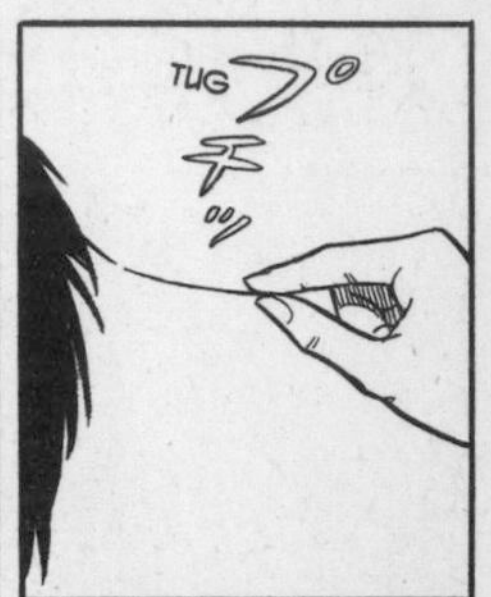
TUG

OW...

OH. IT'S YOU.

NOTHING HAPPENED.

OH... AH HA...
AH HA HA! JUST IGNORE ME.

WAIT A SEC!

HE WAS
SHIMADA
HIDEO,
RIGHT?

SO, THAT
WEIRD
GUY...

JUST...
I DIDN'T
KNOW
WHAT HE
WAS.
IT SEEMED
LIKE YOU
KNEW HIM...

SO DON'T
LOOK LIKE
YOU'RE
GONNA
CRY!

COURSE NOT!
NOBODY
KNOWS
MONSTERS!

......

THIS GIRL IS DIFFERENT... IF I TOLD HER EVERYTHING...

MIGI'S... AWAKE.

SHINICHI... I KNOW WHAT YOU'RE THINKING.

......

BUT SHE IS NO FRIEND OF MINE.

KANA.
YEAH!?

......

YOU ONCE SAID YOU HAD A MYSTERIOUS FEELING ABOUT THINGS?
YEAH! IT'S BUGGING ME, TOO.

EVERY NOW AND THEN I GET THAT FEELING... FROM PEOPLE OTHER THAN YOU.
.........!

SO...I MEAN... I MEAN...YOU CAN'T...
?

YOU CAN'T GO NEAR THEM.

WHY? ARE THEY ALL MONSTERS?
HOW WOULD YOU KNOW THAT?

I MEAN, YOU'RE NORMAL, AREN'T YOU?

RIGHT! THEN I'LL JUST HAVE TO PLUCK ONE OF THEIR HAIRS!

DON'T DO THAT!!

......

WHAT ARE YOU SHOUTING ABOUT?
HOW COULD I DO THAT TO SOMEONE I DON'T EVEN KNOW?

EVERYONE'S GETTING ALL STRESSED OUT... I MEAN, I GET IT WITH YOUR SCHOOL.
WHAT WITH EVERY-THING THAT HAPPENED THERE, BUT...

LIGHTEN UP!
PAT

......

OH, I JUST REMEMBERED!

SHINICHI, SLIP AWAY. WE NEED TO TALK.

SORRY, GOTTA RUN!
....

DON'T TALK TO HER ANY-MORE.
IT'S NOT THAT EASY.

IF ONLY I COULD JUST EXPLAIN IT BETTER...
THEN SHE'D BE SAFER THAN ANYONE.

STILL, EVERY-THING YOU SAY TO HER IS FULL OF HOLES.

MM? YOU'RE...

I'LL BE CARE-FUL.
I WON'T LET HER KNOW ABOUT YOU.
OF COURSE.

HI.
Y-YOU...
YOU WERE RIGHT BEHIND ME? WHY DIDN'T YOU SAY ANYTHING?

YOU'RE MAKING ME FEEL GUILTY OVER NOTHING!

BUT IF YOU AREN'T MORE AGGRESSIVE, YOU'LL LOSE HIM.

......

UM...
I KNOW THIS IS A STRANGE QUESTION, BUT...

EH? WHAT?

DO YOU THINK HE'S CHANGED A LOT?

CHANGED? SINCE WHEN?
I MEAN, I DON'T SEE HIM ALL THAT OFTEN, NOT LIKE YOU...

SINCE YOU FIRST MET HIM.

......

HE'S NOT LIKE HE WAS. I MEAN, IF YOU TALK TO HIM HE'S NORMAL, BUT...

BUT YOU LIKE HIM, RIGHT?

ARE YOU GUYS FIGHT-ING?
......

HE SAVED MY LIFE.

UM... NEVER MIND!

DREAM?

SERI-OUSLY?
WOW, YOU HAD THAT DREAM, TOO?

I DON'T KNOW.
MAYBE HE WAS ALWAYS LIKE THAT.

HE JUST... SEEMS LIKE SOMEONE SPECIAL.

......

LOOKS LIKE I HAVE A CHANCE!

HOTEL BATHS

OW.
TUG
プチッ

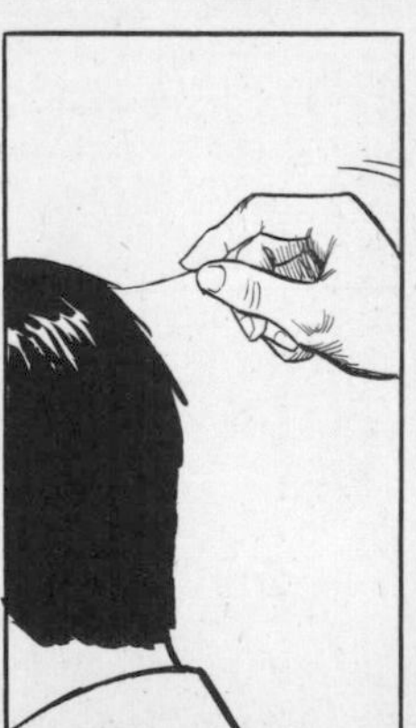

BATHS

SORRY ABOUT THAT, UDA.
YOU JUST SEEMED A LITTLE MORE HIGH STRUNG THAN THE OTHERS...

......

......

D-DO I SEEM LIKE THE TYPE TO YOU?

I HEAR YOU TALK TO YOURSELF SOMETIMES... AND SOMEONE SAID THEY'D SEEN YOUR MOUTH GET REALLY BIG AND SPROUT FANGS. BUT PEOPLE WILL SAY ANYTHING!

OF COURSE NOT! YOU'RE DOING A GREAT JOB HERE!

AH HA HA HA HA HA!
PLEASE...

SIGH...
CLICK

GLLLP

MMM... BUT I HOPE HE'S WELL.
EVERYTHING THAT'S HAPPENED TO HIM MUST BE TAKING ITS TOLL...

YOU CAN'T LET YOUR GUARD DOWN.

I DUNNO...HE SEEMS A LOT STRONGER MENTALLY THAN THE LIKES OF YOU.

BUT THAT THING ABOUT THE HAIR HELPS PEOPLE LIKE YOU AND SHINICHI.

THE LIKES OF ME!?
PEOPLE EVERYWHERE PULLED EACH OTHER'S HAIR OUT...BUT IN MOST CASES, NOTHING HAPPENED.

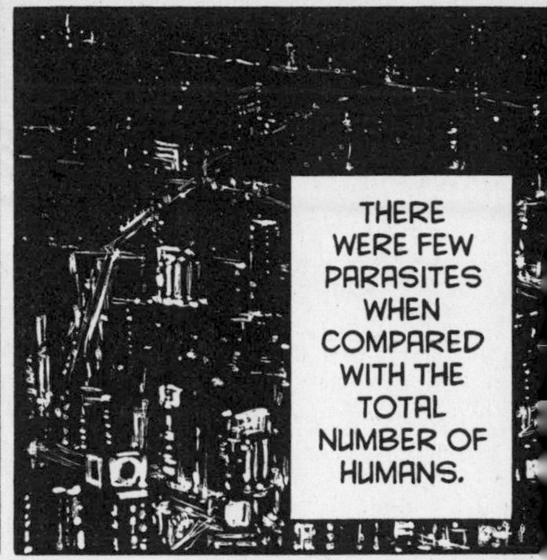
THERE WERE FEW PARASITES WHEN COMPARED WITH THE TOTAL NUMBER OF HUMANS.

BUT OCCASIONALLY...
YOU'RE SO FUNNY, KATO-SAN! MMM? WHY CAN'T I WALK STRAIGHT?

AND WHERE ARE WE?

THE PARK. I THOUGHT THE FRESH AIR WOULD DO YOU GOOD.
ヒク HIC

EH!? HEY, YOU AREN'T KATO! WHAT'S GOING ON?

SORRY...
YOU JUST GRABBED MY ARM SUDDENLY...

AH HA! HA HA HA! WHOOPS!
I THINK I'VE HAD ONE TOO MANY!

YOU KNOW, YOU'RE MUCH BETTER LOOKING THAN KATO.

ARE YOU OKAY? IF YOU GO THAT WAY, THERE'S A SUBWAY ENTRANCE...

I'D BETTER BE...
WAAAIT!

......
WHAT'S YOUR HURRY?

MMM...YOU DO HAVE A PRETTY FACE.
A LITTLE TOO PRETTY! YOU HAD SURGERY, DIDN'T YOU?

HA HA HA! YOU GOT ME.

IT'S LIKE A LIE!
HIC

YOU HEARD ABOUT THIS?
?

TUG
AH!

WHOOPS! I GOT THREE OF THEM...

....

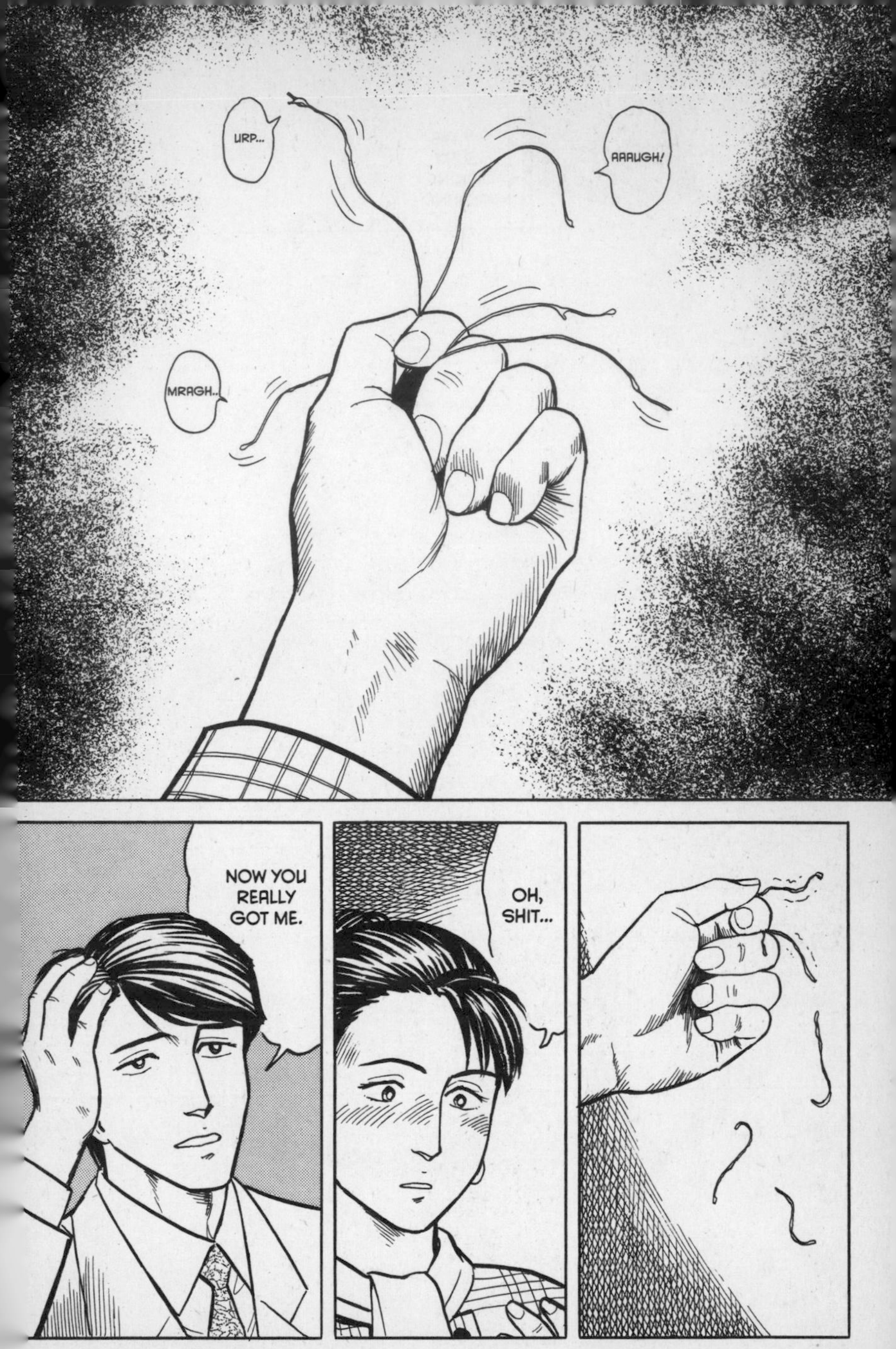

URP...

AAAUGH!

MRAGH...

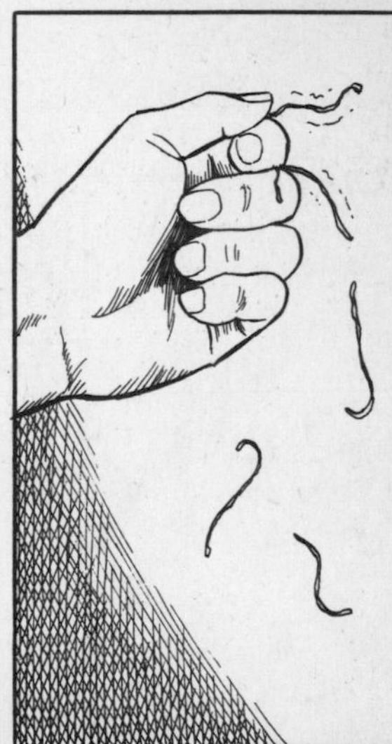

I...I NEVER THOUGHT IT WAS REAL...
I WAS JUST JOKING AROUND!

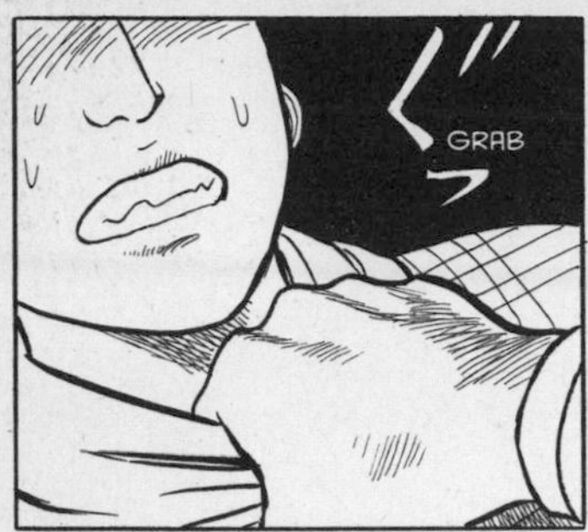
GRAB

STOP, PLEASE! I DIDN'T SEE ANYTHING! I SWEAR! I'M TOO DRUNK!
SILENCE.

NOOOOO!

SQUISH

EEEK!

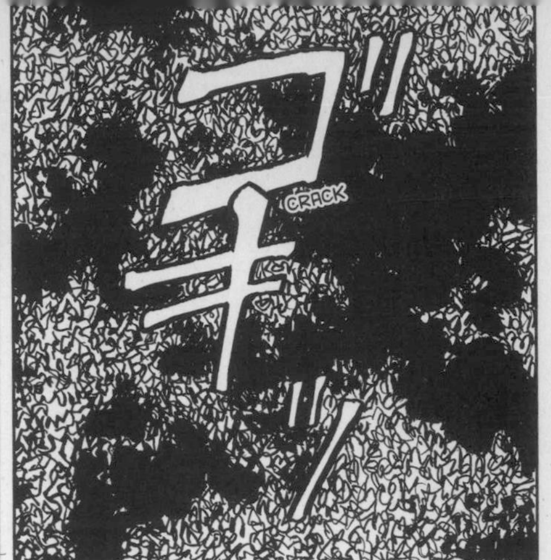
ゴキッ
CRACK

……

RUSTLE
ガサッ

WHAT ARE YOU DOING?

GOOD THING YOU WERE CLOSE BY.
CAN YOU HELP ME?

ALCOHO
YEAH... NOT A LOT, THOUGH.

PLEASE. SHE FIGURED IT OUT SUDDENLY.

YOUR HAIR?
YEAH.

YEAH...BUT SHE WAS DRUNK. DRUNK PEOPLE OFTEN MAKE PASSES AT STRANGERS.

STRANGE. USUALLY THEY ONLY DO THAT WITH PEOPLE THEY KNOW.

I'LL NEVER LEARN TO LIKE ALCOHOL. DRINK A LITTLE OF THAT AND NO MATTER HOW HARD YOU TRY TO KEEP YOUR FACE NORMAL, IT STARTS TO BEND OUT OF SHAPE.

I'LL BE MORE CAREFUL.

MUNCH

MUNCH

KNAW

KNAW

HAPTER 26: THE END

CHAPTER 27: MANEUVERS

THIS IS FINE. STOP HERE.

SKEE...

I'LL WALK THE REST OF THE WAY.

THIS IS EASY TO MOVE IN. AND IT'LL JUST GET DIRTY, ANYWAY.

OKAY, BUT COULDN'T YOU HAVE DRESSED A LITTLE MORE NORMALLY?

I'LL BE BACK IN FIFTEEN OR TWENTY MINUTES.

TRUE ENOUGH

WHAT?

HOW MANY INSIDE?

...LIKE YOU...
GUYS...
CRACK

......

YOU *YAKUZA* CERTAINLY ARE AGGRESSIVE.

EEK!
...LOOK SO HAPPY I JUST GET THE ITCH TO TEACH 'EM A LESSON.

PAY CLOSE ATTENTION.

SPLAT

WHO THE...!?

CLANG

OUT-SIDE?

!?

SPLUT

H-HE JUST...

THUD

CLANG

BLAM

CRUNCH
TAP
!?

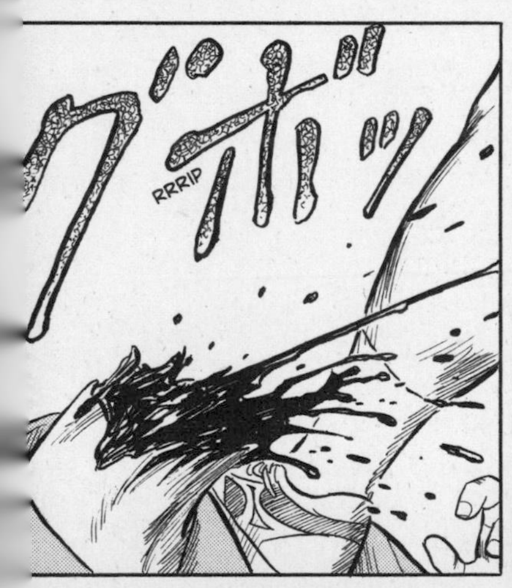
RRRIP

AUGH!

AAUUUGGGHHH!
SP-SPLAAT!

SPLAT

SPLAT

POP!

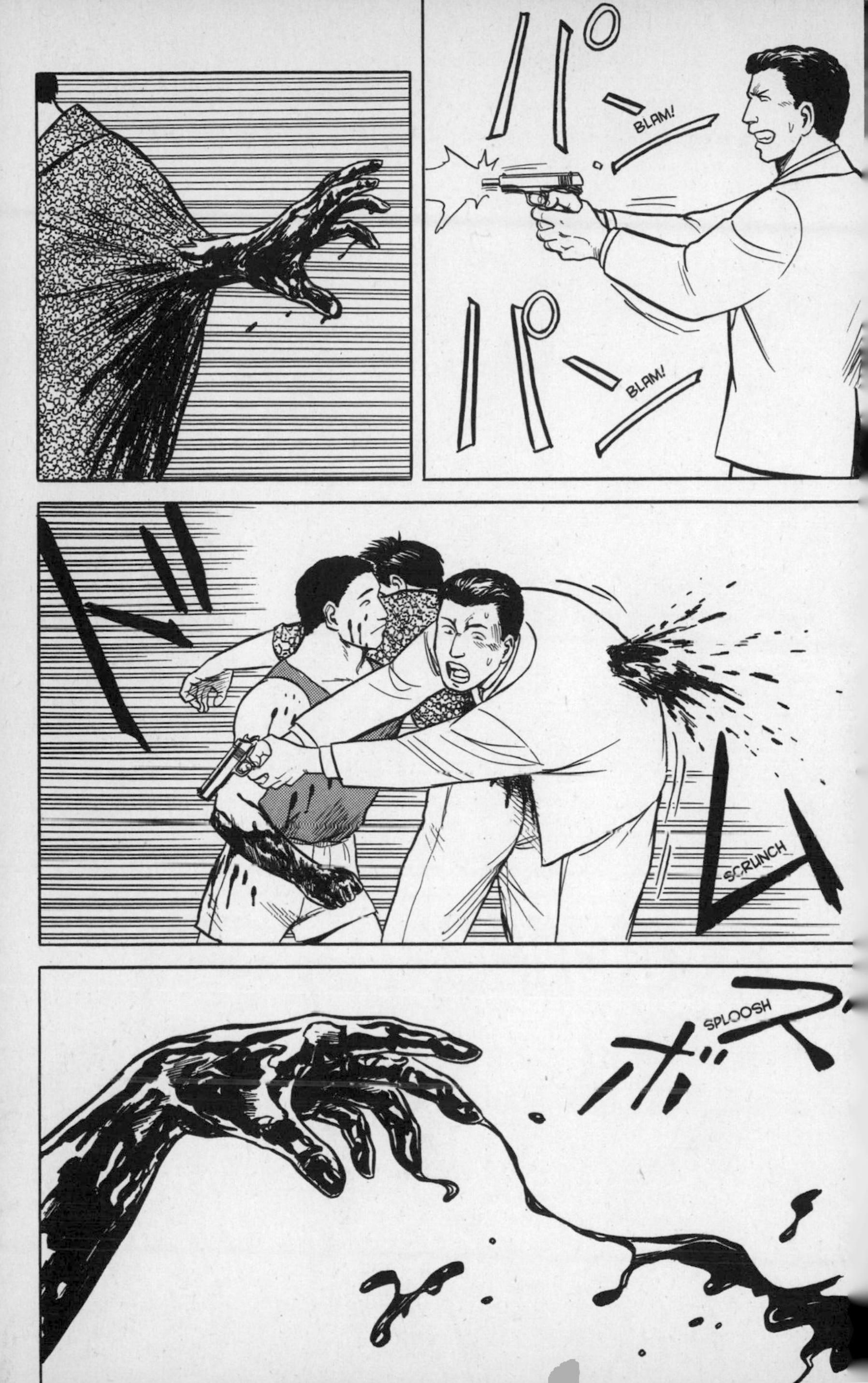
BLAM!
BLAM!
SCRUNCH
SPLOOSH

WHAT'S THE MATTER?

COME ON.
ARRRGH!

CRUNCH
CRACK!

THWACK!

CRUNCH

BOUND

HUNH?
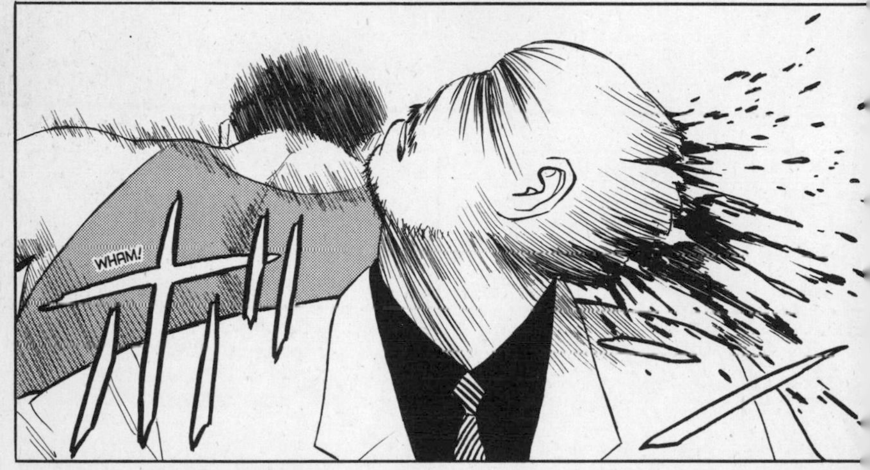
WHAM!

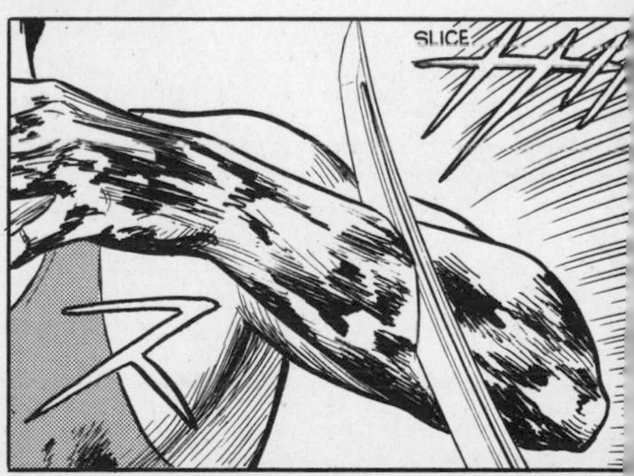
SLICE

CRACK!
!
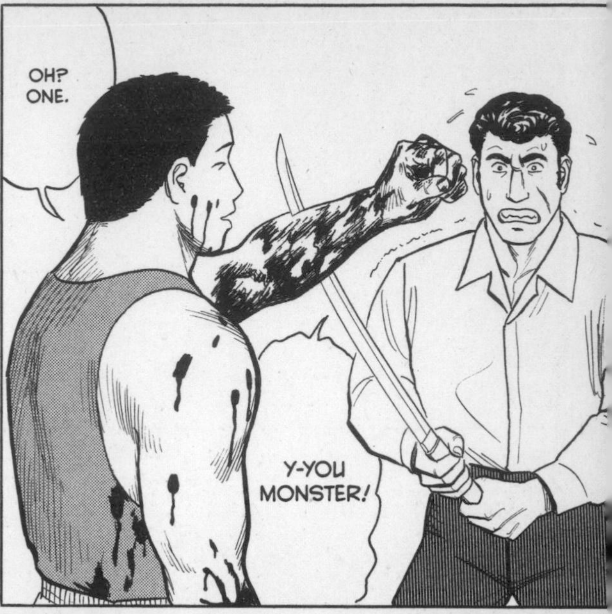
OH? ONE.
Y-YOU MONSTER!

GLLLLP

GLLLP
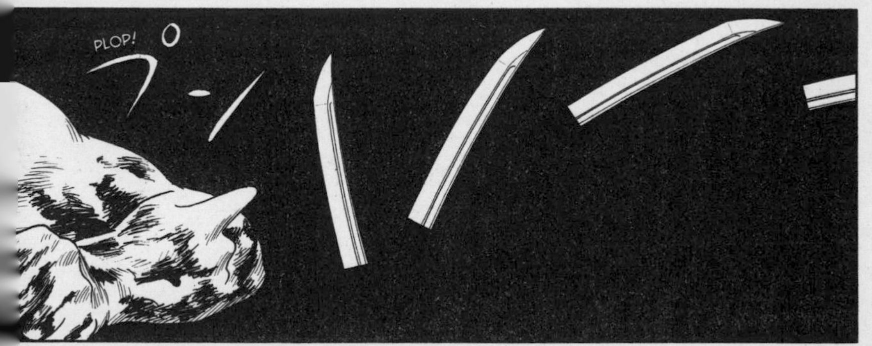
PLOP!

ACK!

パ
BLAM
パ
BLAM

TWO...

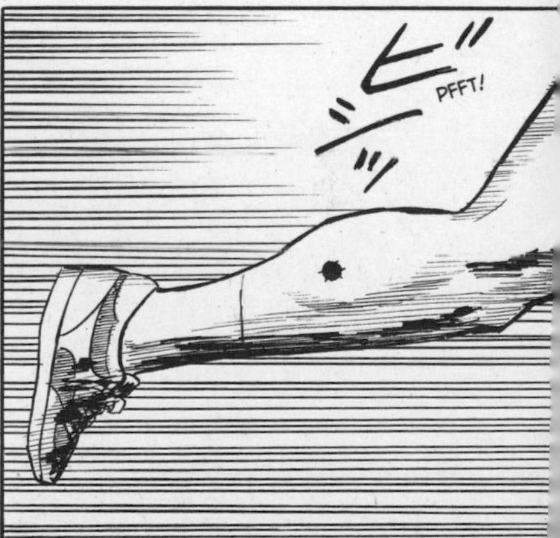
ビ
PFFT!

SCRUNCH

CRACK

SPLAT

THUNK!

SCHUNK!

HEH HEH!
HEH...
GOT HIM!

EEEEEEK!

AND THAT'S THREE.

AAAAAUGH!

I-IMPOSSIBLE.

......
YIKES!
I COULDN'T DODGE THREE.
NOT TOO SHABBY, I GUESS.

UNH!

GUH!
SWISH!

ANYONE LEFT?

AUGH!
THUNK!

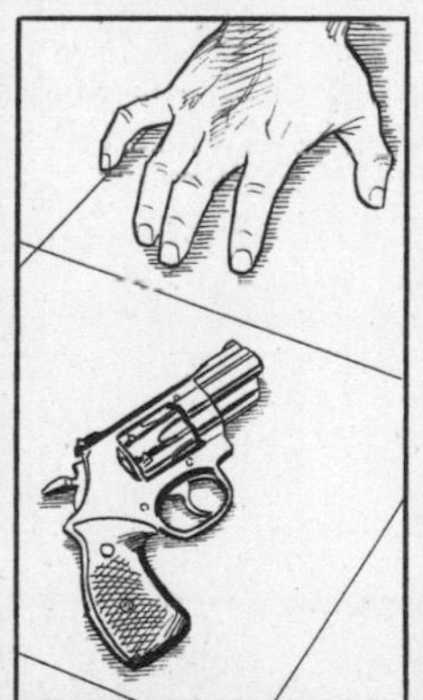

DAMN IT!

THIS WAS AN EXPERIMENT. I THINK I DID PRETTY WELL.

WHAT...THE HELL ARE YOU?

THERE WAS NO ONE ELSE AROUND WHO COULD FIGHT ON THIS SCALE.

AAAAAAH!

WHO PAID YOU TO...

RATTLE

WHAT'S THE CROWD?
A BODY. FACE SMASHED IN, LYING OVER THERE.
GUN-SHOTS FROM INSIDE.

AAUGH!

OH GOD!

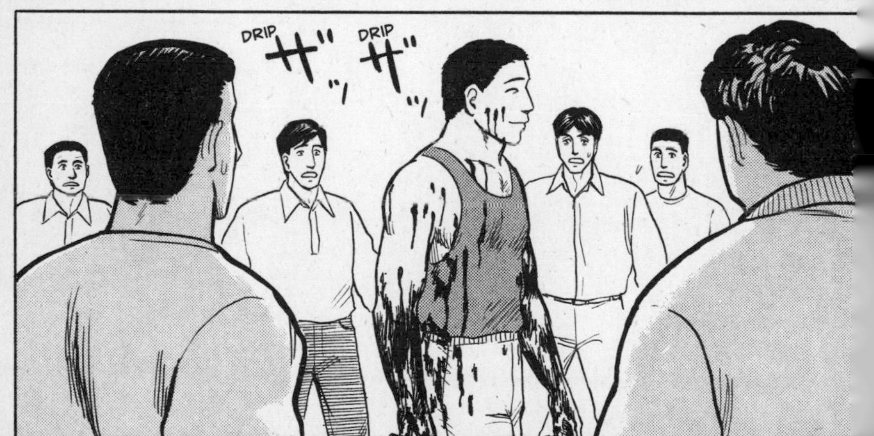

TKK
ダッ
HE'S RUNNING!

AFTER HIM!

WHERE'D HE GO?

TKK TKK TKK
ダダッ

I'M SURE HE WENT THIS WAY.
GIVE IT UP. WE DON'T WANT TO GET MIXED UP IN A YAKUZA WAR.

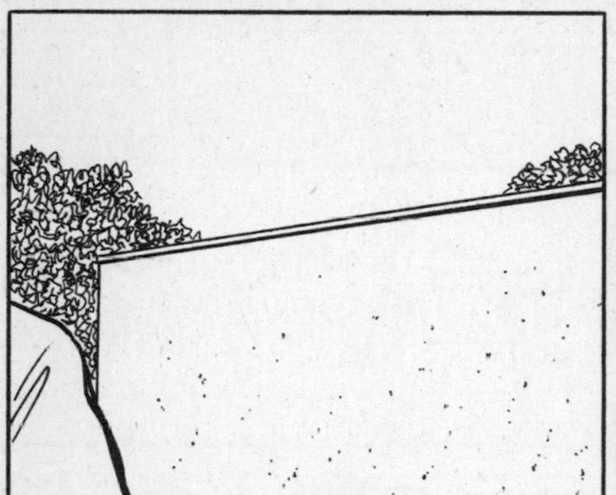

TAP TAP
ARE THE COPS COMING?
DID ANYONE CALL THEM?

SLAM

CLICK
チャッ

……

WHAT?

NOTHING. YOU JUST LOOK DIFFERENT.

BUT NOW I'M DRESSED NORMALLY.
YOU SURE ARE.

VROOOM
ブルルルル

察警
FOR THE MOMENT, IT IS BEING TREATED LIKE A WAR BETWEEN RIVAL GANGS. BUT WITH THE EXCEPTION OF A FEW WHO WERE KILLED WITH A SWORD, MOST OF THE BODIES WERE BEATEN TO A PULP WITH A BLUNT INSTRUMENT—RATHER AN UNUSUAL METHOD OF KILLING. IT MAY BE SOME TIME BEFORE THE EXACT NUMBER OF ASSAILANTS, OR THEIR REAL PURPOSE, IS KNOWN.
ON SALE
¥108000

KILLED THEM ALL, HUNH? WOW.
ールナス

BUT THAT'S NOT HOW THE PARASITES USUALLY KILL...
......

EEEK!

......?

......
EH HEH HEH HEH...

YOU SCARED THE CRAP OUT OF ME!

WHAT? STILL WATCHING?
JUST A LITTLE...

POLICE HEADQUARTERS HELD A PRESS CONFERENCE A FEW MINUTES AGO.

THEY TOOK STATEMENTS FROM EVERYONE WHO SAW A SUSPICIOUS MAN FLEEING THE SCENE, AND THEY HOPE TO RELEASE A MONTAGE PHOTOGRAPH IN THE NEAR FUTURE.
......
MONTAGE, HUNH?

SEEN TAMURA REIKO RECENTLY?

MATER-NITY LEAVE.

OH, RIGHT.

HAPTER 27: THE END

From the Monthly Afternoon Readers' page....

PARASYTE 4 vol. 7

THE READERS ASK THE AUTHOR ANSWERS

"Every line of dialogue hits me right in the heart. 'I sometimes wonder if you're...made of iron.' So sad!"
(Kyoto Prefecture, Opera Guy, 18, Student)

"When writing dialogue, I'm very careful to keep it from becoming unnatural. I don't want to make the story serve the nifty dialogue but let the dialogue arise naturally out of the story. Hopefully I'll be able to keep writing dialogue that makes that kind of impact without ever seeming out of place."
(Hitoshi Iwaaki)

(From *Afternoon*, June 1990)

"I loved the creepy smile Doctor Yui gave on the cover page—the perfect mad scientist. Looking forward to seeing him in action."
(Hyogo Prefecture, IQ1300, 18, Student)

"I'm sure I'm not the only person who thought the doctor's eyes looked far more sinister than Shinichi's."
(Hyogo Prefecture, Yakugami Shusa, 18, Student)

"I think people are often at their most beautiful when throwing themselves into something, but sometimes they wind up, like Yui-sensei, a little too obsessed, and become oblivious to their surroundings. This makes them frightening instead. If we are to make a better society, we have to spend time listening to those who live in slightly different worlds from our own. The right wing, the left wing, religious types and science enthusiasts, all of them need to avoid becoming inhuman."
(Hitoshi Iwaaki)

(From *Afternoon*, November 1991)

From the Monthly Afternoon Readers' page....

PARASYTE 4

vol. 8

THE READERS ASK, THE AUTHOR ANSWERS

"I want to stress that I'm not taking next month off because I've been fighting with my editors. I don't plan Parasyte one chapter at a time, but depending on the complexity of the story, I'll write a very detailed script for three or maybe five issues at a time. But the story starting next issue is especially long, so I need some extra time to work out all the details. Thank you for your understanding."
(Hitoshi Iwaaki)

(From *Afternoon*, April 1992)

"Humans often commit suicide, but the parasites are desperate to stay alive, no matter what. I sometimes wonder if humans are one of the weakest forms of life, mentally."
(Ishikawa Prefecture, Bajou Seijin, 19, Student)

"Certainly, nothing good ever came of suicide, but I believe this mental frailty is part of what makes humanity so appealing. If you're writing a story about a brave hero, the weaker he is inside, the more dramatic his bravery becomes. Characters who start out strong remain strong, and so we never see them become brave."
(Hitoshi Iwaaki)

(From *Afternoon*, June 1992)

CHAPTER 28: A CALM DAY

I STILL DREAM ABOUT IT.

WHEN IT HAPPENS, I REALLY...CAN'T STOP SHAKING, EVEN AFTER I WAKE UP. DOES THAT EVER HAPPEN TO YOU, IZUMI-KUN?

SURE. BUT WHEN MORNING COMES, I'VE ALMOST FORGOTTEN IT...

LUCKY.

MY DREAMS ARE ALWAYS IN COLOR... AND I REMEMBER EVERY DETAIL.

......
YOU'LL BE FINE. EVENTU-ALLY.

......

A FRIEND OF MINE SAID...

IF YOU THINK OF HUMANS AS EQUAL TO COWS, OR PIGS, OR FISH...
THEN HUMANS ARE EATING BITS OF CHOPPED-UP ANIMALS EVERY DAY.

SO WHY SHOULD WE BE FRIGHTENED?

HUNH.

YOUR FRIEND'S A REALLY WEIRD PERSON.

PERSON? YEAH...

MAYBE IT'S HIS FAULT... THE WAY YOU'VE CHANGED.

I DON'T... THINK IT'S THAT SIMPLE.

AH! SORRY!
I DIDN'T MEAN TO BE RUDE!

IT ALL STARTED THEN...

......

IT'S LIKE IZUMI-KUN STILL HASN'T RETURNED...
FROM HIS JOURNEY.

I-IZUMI-KUN...THAT TIME YOUR FATHER WAS HURT ON VACATION...
ガタ
CLATTER

LET'S GO.

......

THOUGHT SO. I'M NOT ALLOWED TO ASK.

COME HERE!

HOW CUTE!

RUN

TKK
TKK
TKK
TKK

WHOAH!

HIS MOM?
LOOKS LIKE IT

ARE THEY STRAYS? NO, SHE'S GOT A COLLAR...

IZUMI-KUN...

SUCH A NICE DAY! NOT TOO HOT, NOT TOO COLD.
STOP IT, YOU SOUND LIKE AN OLD MAN!

MOMMY!
SIGH...

MOMMY!
MOMMY!

COME ON...

I HATE YOU!

YOU CAN DO IT!
MOMM

COME ON!

I HATE YOU, MOMMY!

WHY DO YOU HATE ME?

MOMMY!

WHY?

......

I'M JUST...
I NEED...

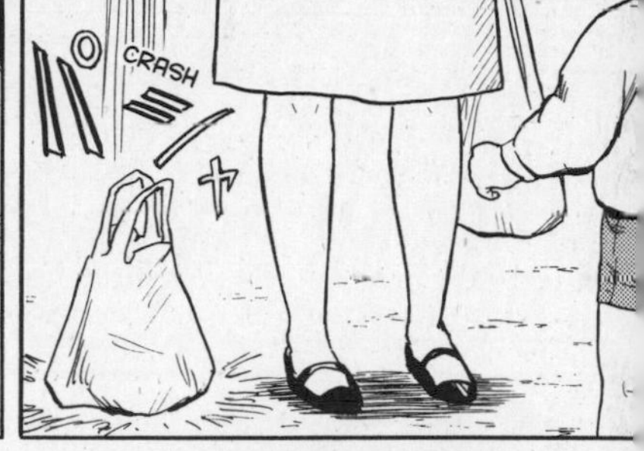
CRASH

IZUMI-
KUN?
HAHH

A-ARE
YOU
OKAY?
HAHH
HAHH

THE HOLE...
THE HOLE
OPENED...

EH?
OH...

THE HOLE?

N- NOTHING. I'M JUST OUT OF BREATH.

WHAT'S WRONG?
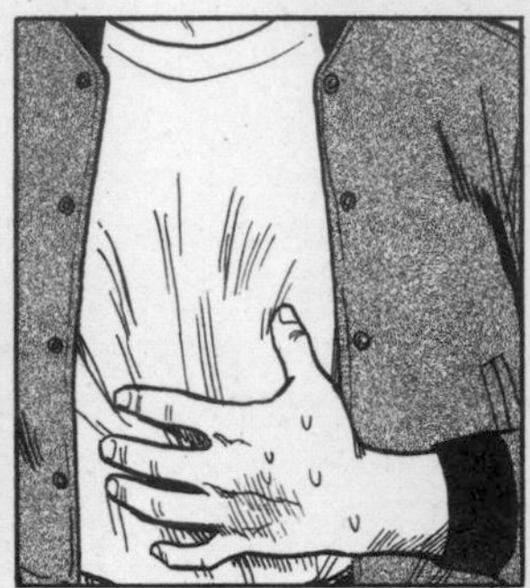

......

......

OH, COME OFF IT!

I MUST BE GETTING OLD.

SOME-TIMES, IT FEELS LIKE MY BODY'S ABOUT TO TEAR ITSELF APART.

BUT THEN, A FEW MINUTES LATER, IT PASSES.

AT TIMES LIKE THAT, I'M SURE THAT PART OF MIGI HAS MINGLED WITH MY MIND, BUT I DON'T KNOW IF THAT'S A GOOD THING OR NOT.

BUT I LIKE THIS GIRL. SHE'S IMPORTANT TO ME.
AND I KNOW THAT FEELING BELONGS ENTIRELY TO ME.

WHEN I'M WITH HER...

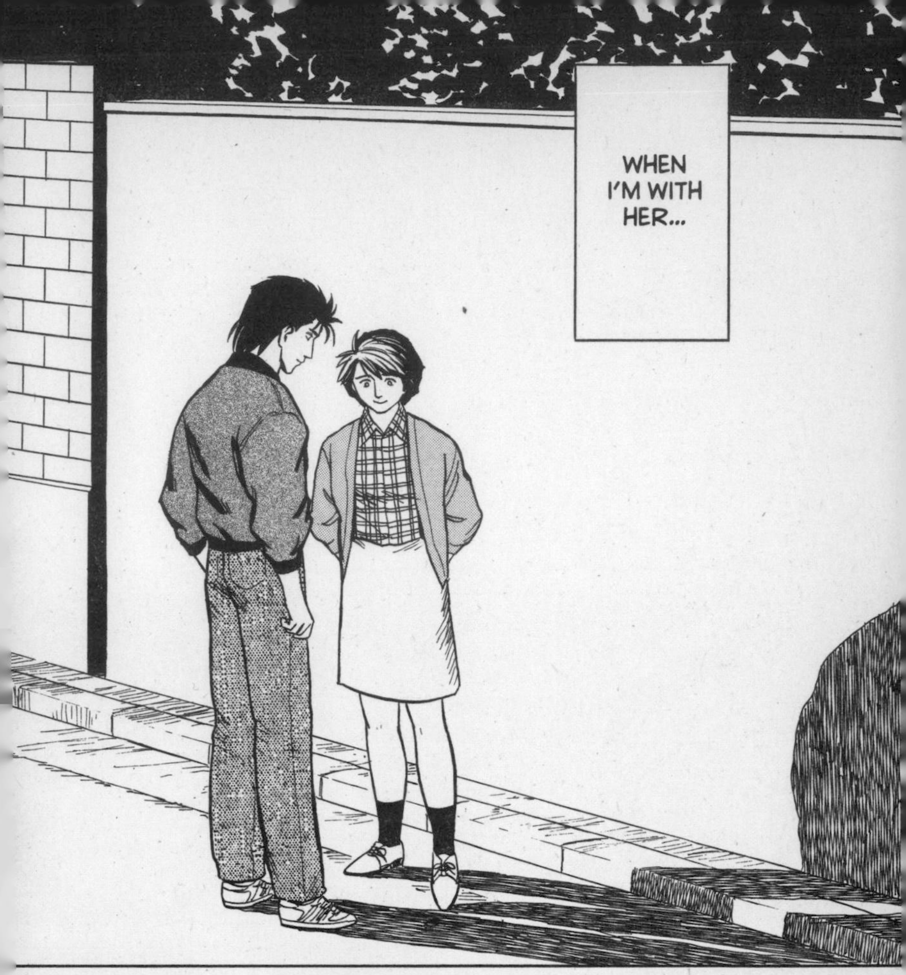

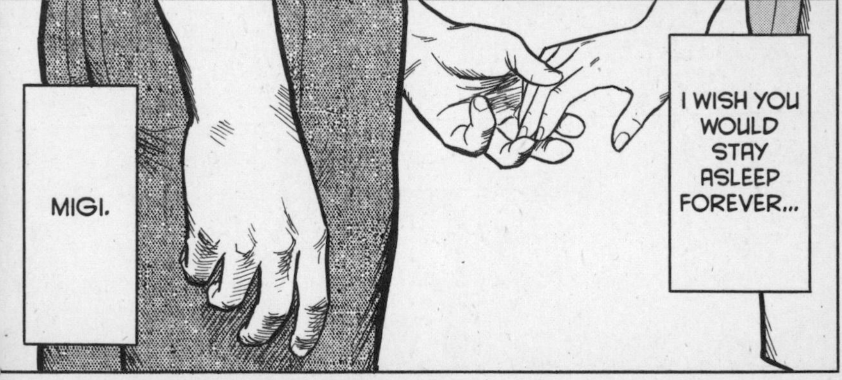
MIGI.
I WISH YOU WOULD STAY ASLEEP FOREVER...

YOU ARE...

IZUMI... SHINICHI, RIGHT?

...GROWN CLOSER TO YOU SOONER...

WOULD STILL...
...BE SURE THAT YOU WERE YOU?

TODAY WAS PEACEFUL, TOO.
SCREECH

SHINICHI.

WAIT FOR THE NEXT ONE.
WHY?

MY KIND ARE ON THE CAR IN FRONT OF US... TWO OF THEM.

!

......
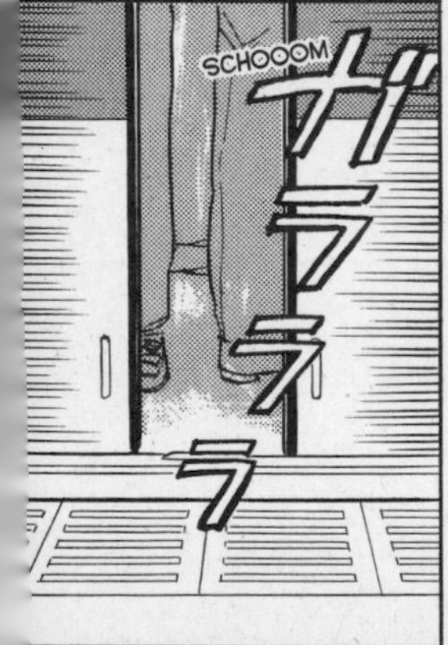
SCHOOOM

TWO AT ONCE?

WHY DO WE HAVE TO RUN? LET'S FOLLOW THEM. IF IT COMES DOWN TO A FIGHT, THEN WE CAN KILL THEM.
WHY DID YOU GET ON?

BUT THEY AREN'T MOVING. NOT INTERESTED IN US.

AH...THEY NOTICED US.

WHAT?
I NEVER REALIZED IT BEFORE, BUT WE'RE LIKE ONITARO AND HIS DAD.

MAKE THEM STOP KILLING.
WHY FOLLOW THEM?

HOW UNSPECIFIC. ARE WE FIGHTING OR NOT?

THEY'RE REACTING TO EACH OTHER... TALKING.

WE WON'T FIGHT IF WE CAN AVOID IT.
HUH. WELL, AS LONG AS WE'RE READY TO GET OUT OF HERE, IT MIGHT BE FUN.

I'M NOT DOING THIS FOR *FUN!*
THEY'RE GETTING OFF.

プシュー
PSSSHHH
YIKES...THIS IS ONLY TWO STOPS FROM MY HOUSE!
ガラ
SHOOOM

ばっ
WHOOSH

BETTER HIDE YOUR FACE.

WAIT TILL THERE'S ALMOST TWO HUNDERD METERS BETWEEN US.

RIGHT TURN HERE...NO, AT THE NEXT ONE, SORRY.
WHERE ARE THEY GOING?

WHAT WE NEED TO CHANGE IS OUR VERY WAY OF THINKING.
SOME-ONE'S GIVING A SPEECH?
AH... THERE'S ANOTHER ONE!
WHAT!?

THREE... NO, FOUR... FIVE.
HOW MANY ARE THERE?

NOT SURE...BU THEY'RE WALKING TOWARD THE SPEECH.
......
IT HAS BECOME POPULAR TO TALK ABOUT ENVIRON-MENTAL PROTECTION ON A GLOBAL SCALE, BUT WHAT EFFECT CAN EACH OF US HAVE PERSONALLY? HOW MUCH IMPACT CAN WE REALISTICALLY HAVE? FOR EXAMPLE...

I DON'T DENY THERE ARE MANY RELEVANT ISSUES THAT I'M NOT EXPLORING HERE...

WHAT ARE THEY ALL DOING HERE? LISTENING TO THE SPEECH?
NO CLUE.

BUT WOULD YOU GIVE UP YOUR CARS TO MAKE THE WORLD A LITTLE CLEANER?
OVER THERE?
WAIT!

I'LL LOOK FOR YOU!
NO, WAIT!

WE CAN'T CHANGE YOUR FACE! WE DON'T WANT THEM KNOWING WHAT YOU LOOK LIKE!

NO, WAIT! AT LEAST UNTIL I KNOW HOW MANY, AND WHERE...

WHY DON'T WE JUST HIDE IN THE GROUND AGAIN? IT'S BETTER THAN WAVING YOUR EYES AROUND.

IT IS HUMAN NATURE TO TAKE THE EASIER PATH. WE CAN'T TURN OUR BACK ON CULTURAL ADVANCEMENT. BUT IF WE DO NOTHING, THE ENTIRE WORLD IS IN DANGER.

WE ALLOW OUR FEELINGS TO INFLUENCE US BECAUSE WE LACK A CLEAR VISION OF THE FUTURE.

STILL NOTHING?
THEY'RE GATHERED TOGETHER... THE SIGNALS ARE MINGLING, HARD TO PIN DOWN...

GOT IT! ABOUT SIXTY METERS, UP HIGH...SIX OF THEM ON A PLATFORM OF SOME KIND, TWO MORE DOWN BELOW.
EIGHT?

HIROKAWA TAKESHI FOR MAYOR

ONE METHOD IS TO PAINT A PICTURE OF A TERRIBLE FUTURE, AND THREATEN PEOPLE WITH IT: "THIS IS WHAT THE WORLD WILL BE LIKE!"
BUT WE WOULD PREFER TO PRESENT A VISION OF A BEAUTIFUL UTOPIA, AND SAY, "IF YOU DO THIS, THE WORLD WILL BECOME A WONDERFUL PLACE."
AND, OF COURSE, THAT HAS TO BE A REALISTIC PROPOSITION, ONE THAT EVERYONE WILL BELIEVE IN.
SIX... ALL OF THEM!?

TWO MORE BELOW...BUT FROM THIS DISTANCE, NOT SURE WHO. IF OUR EYES MEET, I'LL KNOW, BUT...

IF WE DO THAT, PEOPLE WILL CEASE TO FOCUS ONLY ON CONVENIENCE, AND THINK ABOUT OTHER OPTIONS...OR AT LEAST BE AWARE THAT THEY EXIST.

YOU MAY THINK THIS IS BIG TALK FOR A LOCAL ELECTION, BUT RIGHT NOW, THESE ISSUES NEED TO BE DEALT WITH AT A LOCAL, RATHER THAN NATIONAL, LEVEL AS REALISTICALLY, EFFECTIVELY, AND CLEARLY AS POSSIBLE.

GOOD GOD! WHAT ARE THEY THINKING?
A PARASITE RUNNING FOR OFFICE?

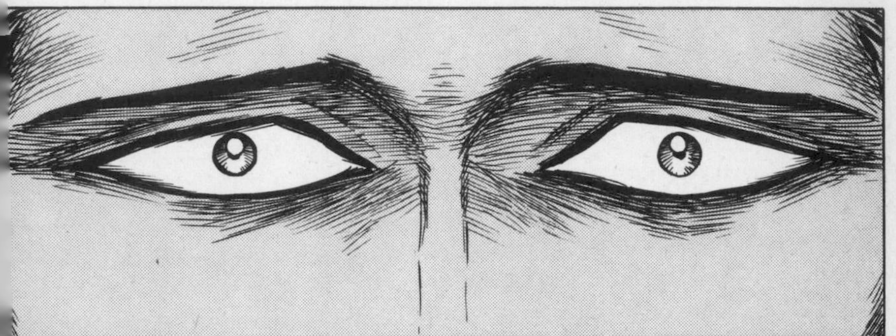

DID HE SEE ME?
NO, I WAS IN THE CROWD.
HE SAW YOU.

YOUR EYES MET. BUT HE DOESN'T SEEM VERY INTERESTED IN YOU—JUST CURIOUS. WE SHOULD LEAVE, THOUGH.

MONSTERS MAKING SPEECHES? WHAT NEXT?
THE ACTIONS OF ONE CITY MIGHT BE SMALL, BUT THERE ARE 500,000 PEOPLE IN THIS CITY. IF WE ALL MOVE TOGETHER WE CAN SHAKE THE EARTH!

AND THEY'RE APPLAUD ING!
CLAP
CLAP
CLAP
CLAP
CLAP
CLAP

!

IZUMI! I THOUGHT SO!

WH- WHAT ARE YOU DOING HERE?

COME ON. I LIVE HERE. WHY ARE YOU HERE?

UH- OH...

HAPTER 28: THE END

CHAPTER 29: KANA

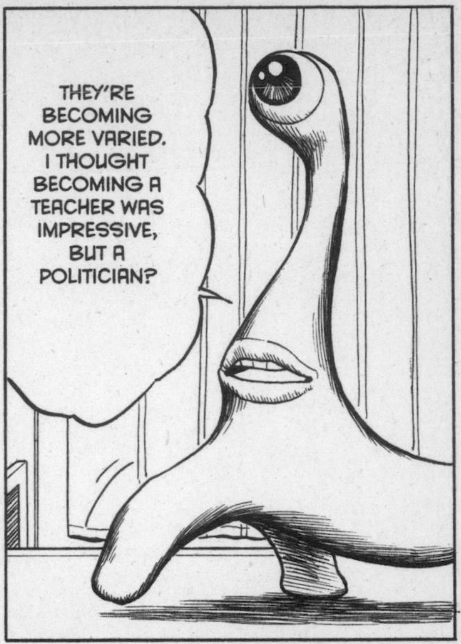
THEY'RE BECOMING MORE VARIED. I THOUGHT BECOMING A TEACHER WAS IMPRESSIVE, BUT A POLITICIAN?

YOU HAVE TO HAVE A PHENOMENAL UNDERSTANDING OF HUMAN MINDS TO GET ELECTED! WHAT ARE THEY AFTER!?

....

THEY'LL NEVER GET ELECTED... THEY'LL GET CAUGHT!
WAIT, THEY'RE IN THE NEXT TOWN OVER...

IT'S WORTH KEEPING AN EYE ON. THEY MUST HAVE DONE THEIR HOMEWORK.

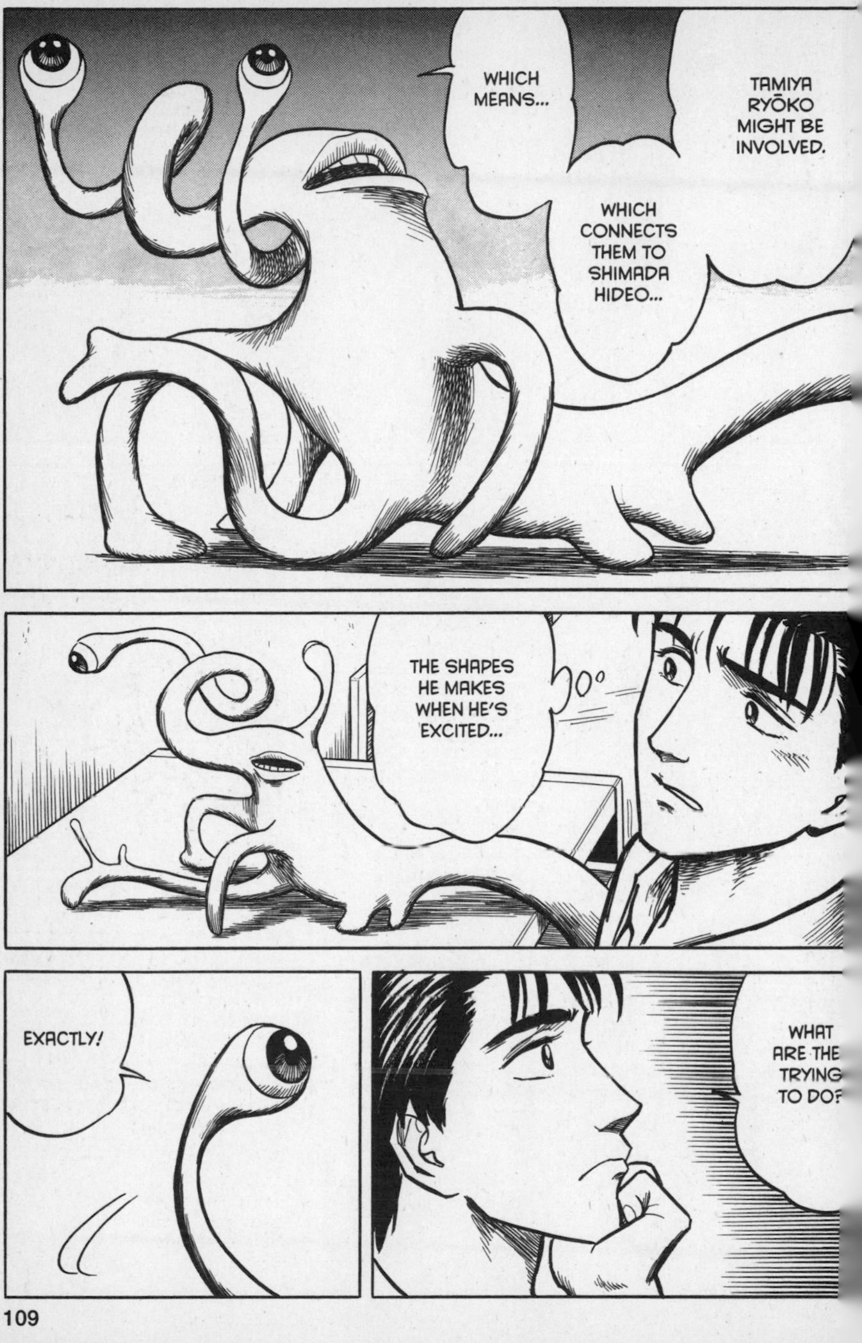

WHICH MEANS...
TAMIYA RYŌKO MIGHT BE INVOLVED.
WHICH CONNECTS THEM TO SHIMADA HIDEO...

THE SHAPES HE MAKES WHEN HE'S EXCITED...

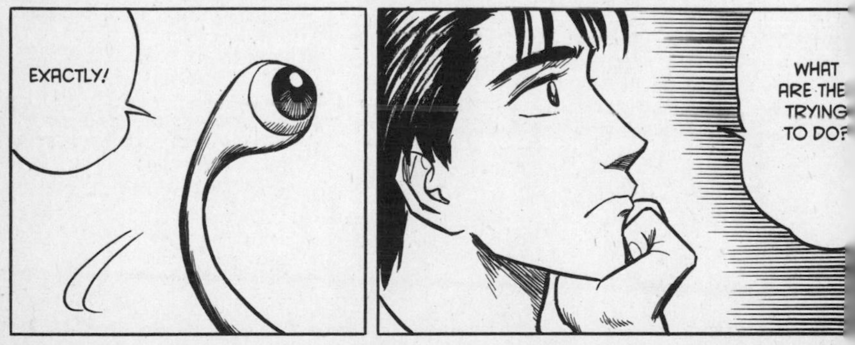

EXACTLY!
WHAT ARE THE TRYING TO DO?

GET REAL.

ONE, THEY HAVE TO BE HUMAN... SO THEY STUDY HUMANS, AND ON THE WAY, BECOME INTERESTED IN POLITICS...THAT WAS A PRETTY GOOD SPEECH.
HE MIGHT END UP BEING A GOOD MAYOR, FOR THE PEOPLE OF THE WORLD.

I FOUGHT A MONSTER!

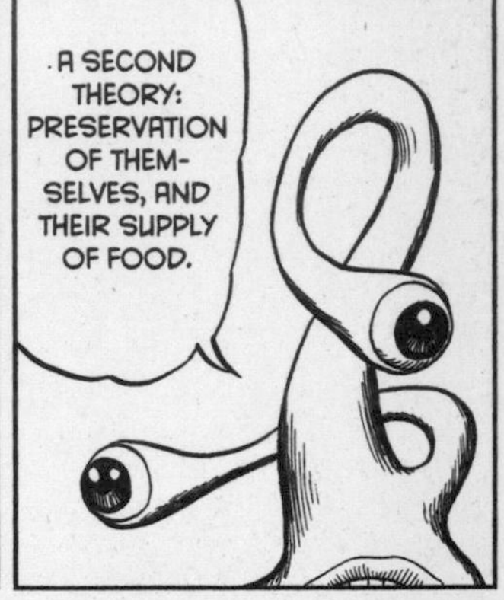
A SECOND THEORY: PRESERVATION OF THEM-SELVES, AND THEIR SUPPLY OF FOOD.
THEY MIGHT BE HIDING THE BODIES THEY FEED ON NOW, BUT EVEN THEN, PEOPLE ARE STILL VANISHING. AND THEY MIGHT OCCASIONALLY KILL SOMEONE FAMOUS...
THAT WOULD CAUSE PANIC.

YOU'RE TALKING TOO FAST FOR ME TO FOLLOW, BUT THE SECOND THEORY SOUNDS RIGHT.
AGREE.

BASICALLY, THEY'D BECOME AUTONO-MOUS.

TO PREVENT THAT, AND KEEP THINGS QUIET, IN ORDER TO SECURE THEIR SUPPLY, BEING ABLE TO SUPERVISE AND MANIPULATE THE DATA OF THOUSANDS OF PEOPLE WOULD BE A BIG HELP.

THERE WERE EIGHT OF THEM THERE. THERE MIGHT BE EVEN MOR
OF THEM.

DEVELOPED?

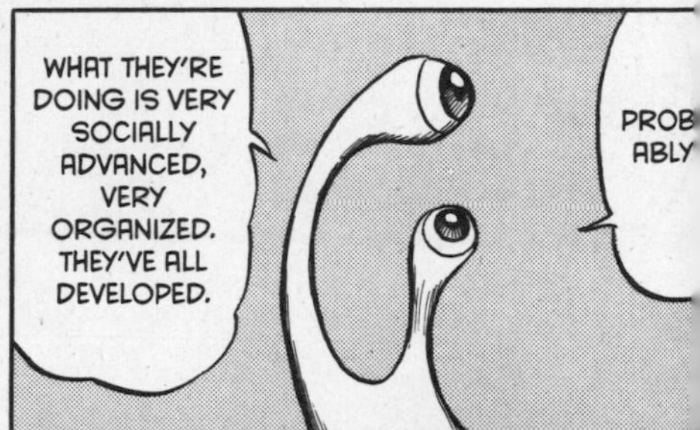
WHAT THEY'RE DOING IS VERY SOCIALLY ADVANCED, VERY ORGANIZED. THEY'VE ALL DEVELOPED.
PROB ABLY

THEN?

IN THE NEXT TOWN.
THEY'R GATHERIN

WHY ARE YOU HERE?
DID YOU COME TO SEE ME?
HA HA!

......

LET'S GET OUT OF HERE.

HUH? WHY?

WHY DID I COME THERE? WELL...
I COULD SENSE THAT YOU WERE THERE.

AND NOT JUST YOU.

IN THE CROWD BEHIND YOU...
THERE WERE FOUR OR FIVE MORE, RIGHT?

......

BUT SHE'S STILL IN DANGER. I CAN'T LEAVE THINGS LIKE THIS!

FOUR OR FIVE... MIGI EVENTUALLY WAS SURE OF EIGHT, SO HER POWER ISN'T AS STRONG AS THEIR OWN ABILITY TO SENSE EACH OTHER.

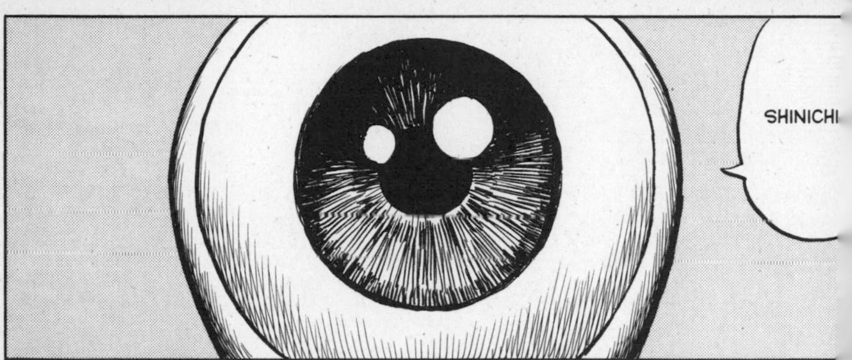
SHINICHI

EEP!

I'LL THINK WHATEVER I WANT! I'M THE HEAD!

WHAT ARE YOU THINKING?
OH, NOTHING...
SCARED ME.

....

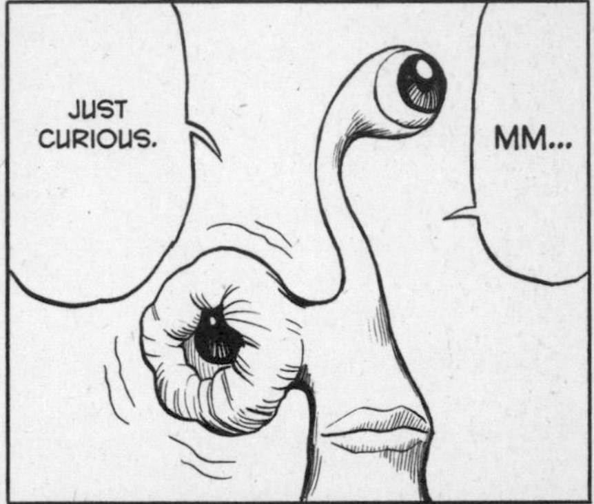
MM...
JUST CURIOUS.

PUT OUR PLANET FIRST!

HIROKAWA TAKESHI

FOR MAYOR

I'D PREFER NOT TO GET INVOLVED. WE COULD NEVER WIN IN A FIGHT.

I'M NOT HERE TO FIGHT.
I JUST WANT TO KNOW HOW MANY THERE ARE.

WE CAN'T COUNT THEM ALL.

WE JUST NEED A GENERAL IDEA.

SEE HOW MANY WE SENSE WALKING BY, WITHOUT GOING NEAR ANY.

YOU'RE INTERESTED IN HOW THEY'RE DEVELOPING AS WELL, RIGHT?

I SUPPOSE.

SO?

YOU CAN'T FIND ANY WHEN YOU GO LOOKING. MUST NOT BE TOO MANY.

MY MY MY!

YOU AGAIN!
YEAH...

WE KEEP BUMPING INTO EACH OTHER.

I KEEP FINDING YOU. YOU KNOW THAT, RIGHT?

......

WE NEED TO TALK, SERIOUSLY.

THESE POWERS YOU MEN-TIONED.

FEELINGS?
YOU EVER FEEL THEM FOR PEOPLE BESIDES ME? ESPECIALLY AROUND HERE?

YEAH...
OCCASIONALLY. THEY LOOK NORMAL...
IT COULD BE SOME BUSINESS-MAN.

......

I'LL SAY IT AGAIN.
WHEN YOU FEEL THAT, PLEASE KEEP AWAY.

BUT WHY
ARE THEY THESE PARASITES EVERYONE'S TALKING ABOUT?

ARE YOU ONE OF THEM?
UH... WELL...

KANA!

MITSUO!

I NEED TO TALK TO HER.

......

OKAY THEN.
NO, WAIT!

NEXT TIME.
I'LL TELL YOU THE EST LATER. CAN I HAVE YOUR NUMBER?

WHAT!?
WHO NEEDS IT?

JUST COME CLOSE TO ME, AND I'LL FIND YOU!

HUNH?

HOW MANY TIMES DO I HAVE TO SAY IT?
IF YOU FEEL IT FOR SOME-ONE BESIDES ME...

FEEL WHAT
KANA!!
OKAY, WE'LL MEET AT THE STATION NEAR SCHOOL.

OKAY, THEN.

I CAN'T TAKE THIS ANY-MORE!

YOU'RE AN IDIOT, MITSUO.
LET'S GO, KANA!
......

SHINICHI...
SHINICHI...

YOU SAID YOU'LL TELL HER THE REST?

WERE YOU REALLY THERE TO SEE HER?
WHAT IF I WAS?

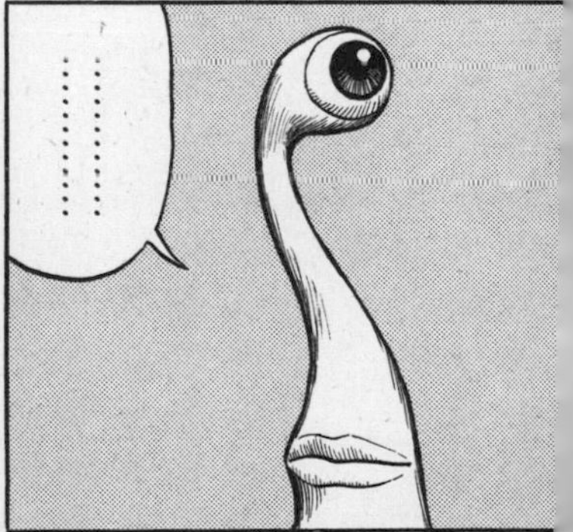
......

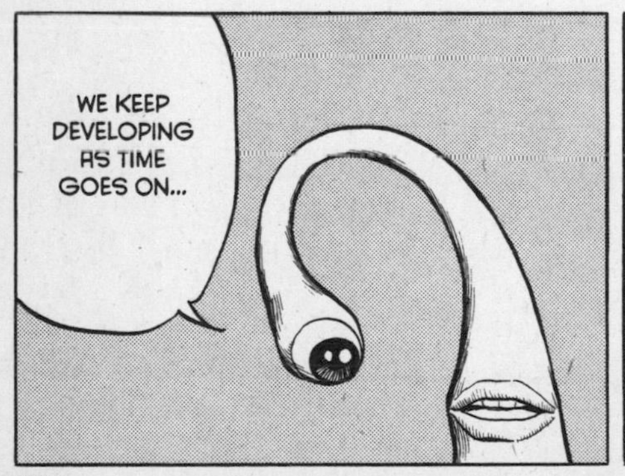
WE KEEP DEVELOPING AS TIME GOES ON...

IF YOU TELL HER ANYTHING LIKE THAT...
AND I WOULD PREFER YOU NOT DO ANY-THING THAT WOULD PUT ME IN DANGER.

BUT WE'VE NEVER DEVELOPED HUMAN FEELINGS.
I KNOW.
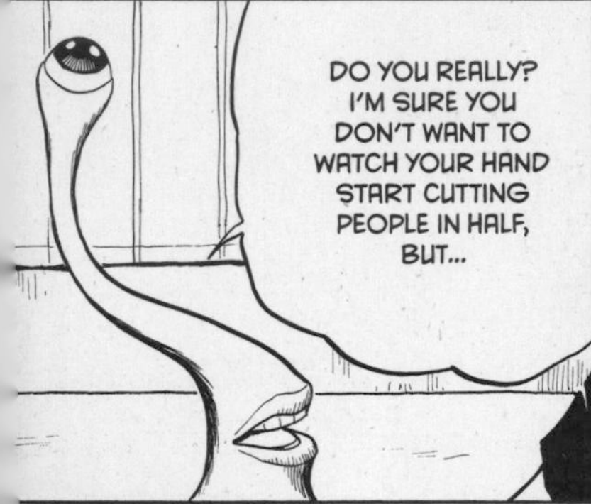
DO YOU REALLY? I'M SURE YOU DON'T WANT TO WATCH YOUR HAND START CUTTING PEOPLE IN HALF, BUT...

I KNOW WHAT YOU MEAN, BUT...

......
......

YEAH.

IS THAT...A THREAT?

YOU REALLY DON'T HAVE A HEART!

THAT'S WHAT I TOLD YOU.

HEH... HEH HEH HEH...

HE'S GONNA TELL ME THE REST?

AGAIN... VERY CLOSE!

I'M SURE IT ISN'T HIM, BUT...

BUT WHY WOULD SHINICHI BE HERE THIS LATE?

JUST IN CASE...

OVER THERE...

AROUND THAT CORNER

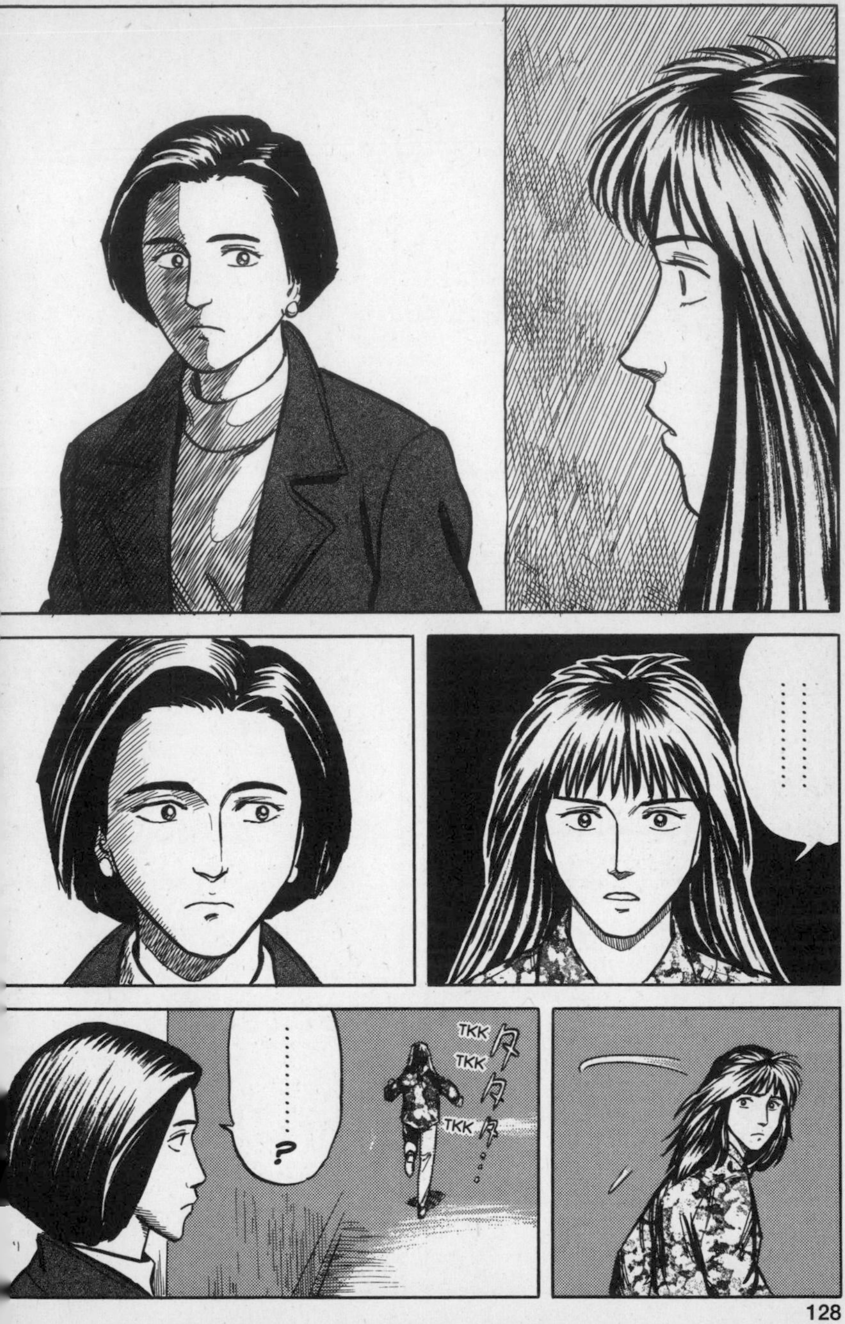

......

TKK
TKK
TKK
......?

IT WAS THE WRONG PERSON... AND A WOMAN.
HUH...

IF ONLY I COULD TELL SHINICHI AND THE OTHERS APART...

THIS WEEKEND?
SURE.

YOU DON'T HAVE TO STUDY?
SPEAK FOR YOURSELF.

WHAT DOES THAT MEAN?
AHHH, WHAT EVER SHALL I DO?

I'VE BEEN LOOKING ALL OVER FOR YOU, BUT...
OH...

ABOUT THAT...

YOU SAID YOU WANTED TO TELL ME SOME-THING?

......

BUT I GUESS NOT NOW.

SO I THOUGHT I'D BETTER HEAR YOU OUT.

I DID, BUT...

SO HERE! MY PHONE NUMBER.
PAT
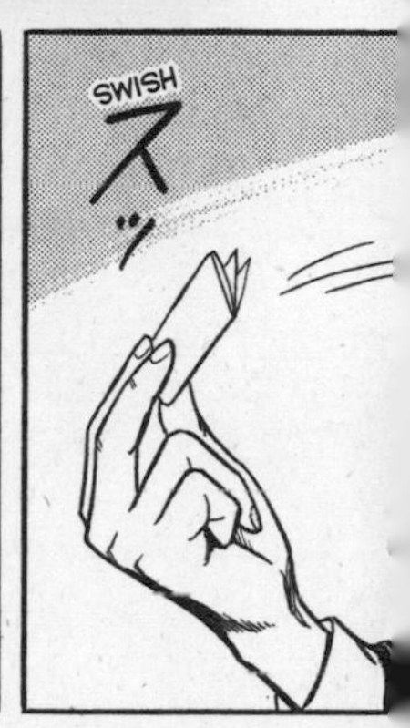
SWISH

ANY TIME.
......

REALLY! IT WAS NOTHING!
REALLY...

UM, THAT WAS JUST...

I BUMPED INTO HER THE OTHER DAY...
DID YOU?

NO, IT'S NOT LIKE THAT!
YOU'VE GOT IT ALL WRONG!

AND THAT BIG GUY FROM NORTH HIGH WAS THERE. I DIDN'T WANT HIM MAKING A PASS AT HER...
UH-HUH.

......

OH, GOD.
HE'S BEEN ODDLY CALM LATELY. THIS SORT OF PANIC IS MUCH MORE LIKE HIM.

HMM...

THE EMERGENCY ELECTION TO FILL THE VACANT SEAT OF THE HIGASHI-FUKUYAMA-SHI MAYOR HAS GONE TO FIRST-TIME CANDIDATE HIROKAWA TAKESHI, WHO DEFEATED THE FORMER DEPUTY MAYOR, IMAI KATSUYUKI.

HIROKAWA TAKESHI (41)

THEY'RE JUST AS SMART AS WE ARE...

HIROKAWA RAN PRIMARILY ON A PLATFORM OF GLOBAL ENVIRONMENTAL PROTECT...

AND THEY'LL DO ANYTHING TO PROTECT THEMSELVES.

IT MIGHT BE SAFER TO NOT KNOW THAT.

BUT NOT FOR KANA!
NOT WITH HER POWER, AND THEM GATHERING IN HER TOWN...

BUT HE HAS A SERIOUS WEAK-NESS. HE SLEEPS FOUR HOURS A DAY.

I HAVE TO TELL HER...
AND MAKE HER UNDER-STAND!

MY ONLY PROBLEM IS MIGI...

YES?
SURE, ANY TIME.

SOME-WHERE PRIVATE.

PRIVATE? UM...

YEAH, I KNOW A PLACE.

HERE...

YEAH, WE COME HERE SOMETIMES.
IT'S USUALLY DESERTED BY DAY.

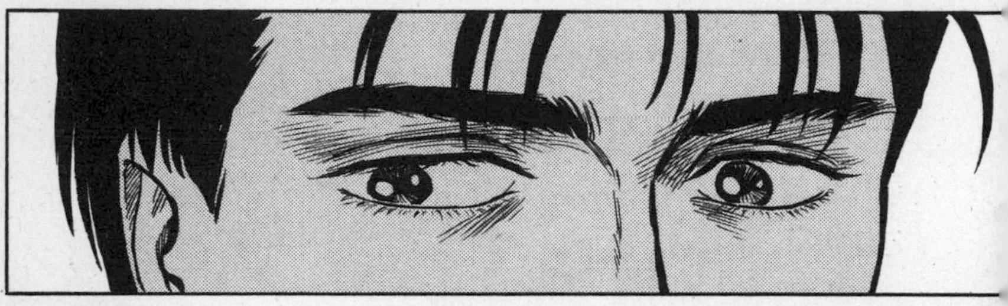

THUNK!

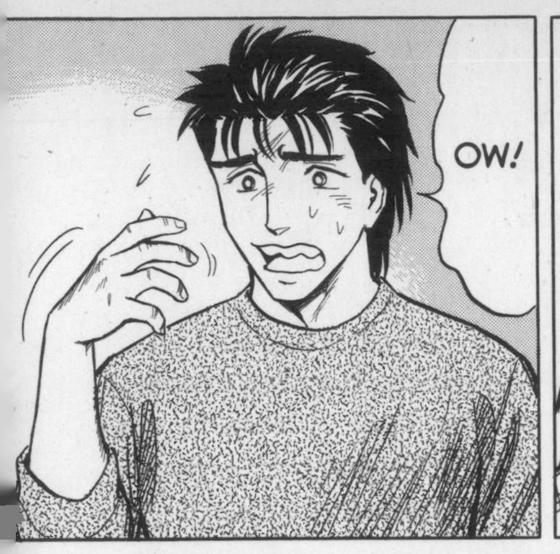

OW!

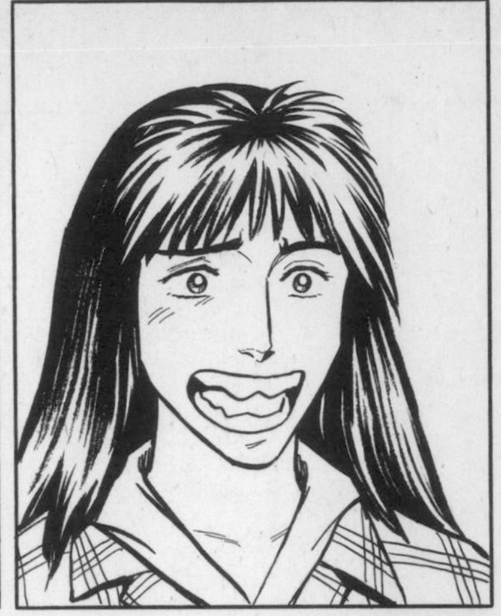

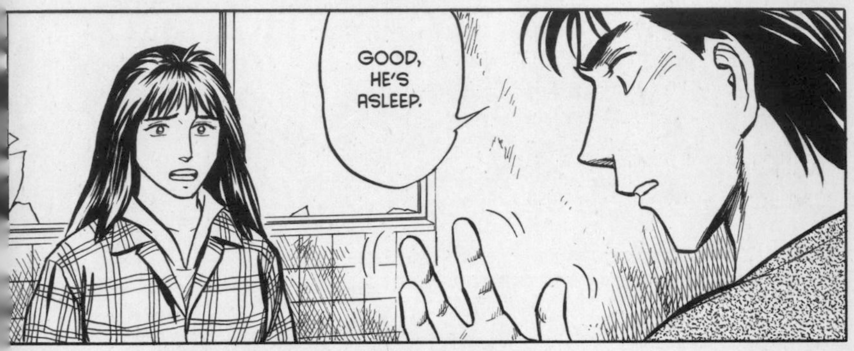

GOOD, HE'S ASLEEP.

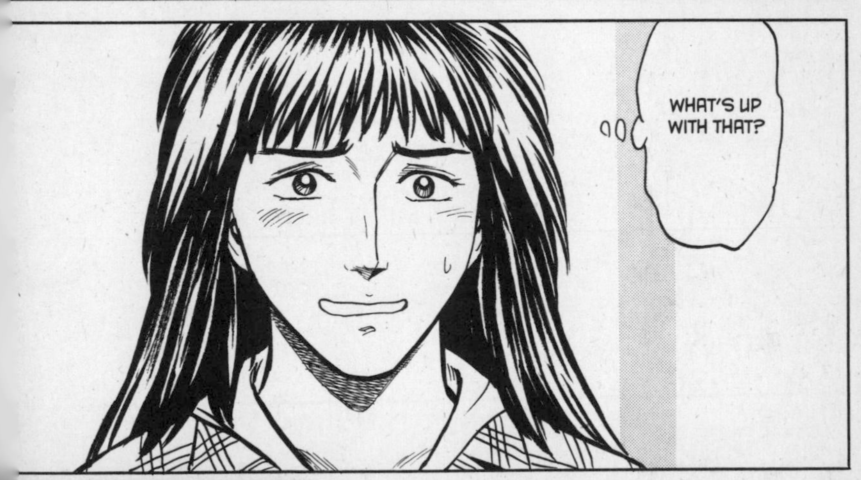

WHAT'S UP WITH THAT?

APTER 29: THE END

CHAPTER 30: POWER

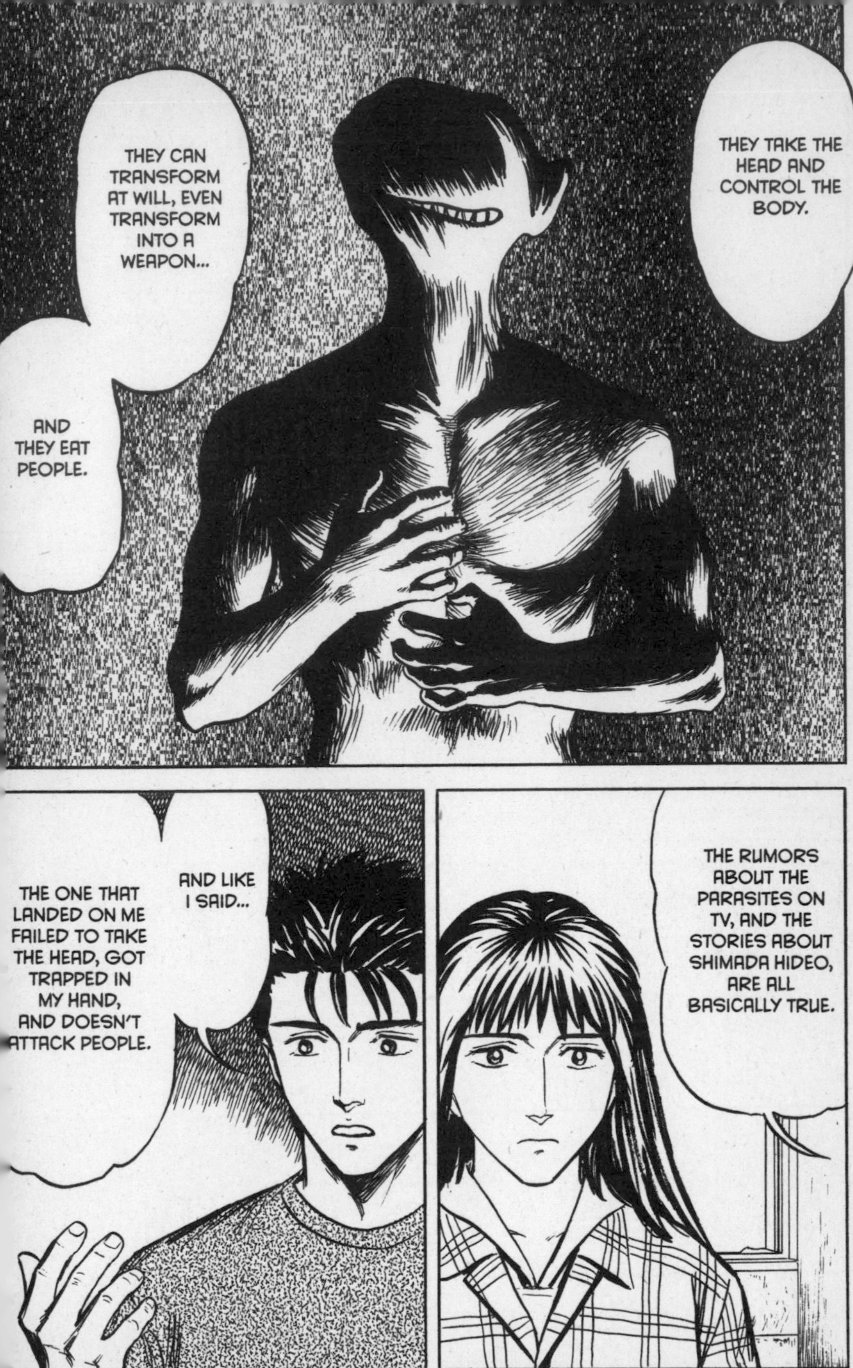

THEY TAKE THE HEAD AND CONTROL THE BODY.
THEY CAN TRANSFORM AT WILL, EVEN TRANSFORM INTO A WEAPON...
AND THEY EAT PEOPLE.

THE RUMORS ABOUT THE PARASITES ON TV, AND THE STORIES ABOUT SHIMADA HIDEO, ARE ALL BASICALLY TRUE.

AND LIKE I SAID...
THE ONE THAT LANDED ON ME FAILED TO TAKE THE HEAD, GOT TRAPPED IN MY HAND, AND DOESN'T ATTACK PEOPLE.

DOES THIS MAKE SENSE?

......

CHEEP
ピィ
CHEEP
ピィ

I WAS HOPING...

YOU WERE GOING TO SAY SOME-THING ELSE.

......

I KNOW THIS IS ALL HARD TO BELIEVE.

BUT EVERY-THING I SAID IS...
IF IT'S TRUE, THEN SHOW ME.
I WANT TO SEE YOU CHANGE.

LIKE I SAID, HE'S ASLEEP NOW. IF HE WAS AWAKE, WE'D BE IN TROUBLE.

GOT A LIGHT?
GUESS NOT.

I MEAN, WOULD I GO TO ALL THIS TROUBLE...
JUST TO LIE TO YOU?

MAYBE YOU'RE PUSHING ME AWAY, BECAUSE MITSUO THREATENED...

...ASKED YOU TO?

FFF...
ふー
THIS IS MORE IMPORTANT THAN THAT!

OR IS IT FOR HER?

HUH.

WHY CAN'T YOU JUST COME OUT AND SAY IT?

JUST SAY YOU DON'T LIKE ME...
JUST TELL ME.

!

KANA... I JUST...

S- SORRY!
!?

THE OTHER DAY YOU WERE WITH THAT GIRL, AND I POPPED OUT AND SAID ALL KINDS OF THINGS...
YOU'RE PISSED ABOUT THAT, AREN'T YOU?

NO, THAT'S NOT...

SORRY! I WON'T DO IT AGAIN.
I'LL STAY AWAY FROM HER.

THIS IS GOING NO-WHERE.
I MEAN, I KNOW I CAN'T PROVE IT, BUT...

MY POINT IS, THE POWER YOU MENTIONED IS THE ABILITY TO DETECT MONSTERS
AND I HAVE ONE OF THEM LIVING IN MY BODY.

OKAY.
MMM?

MONSTERS, RIGHT?

Y-YEAH...

I CAN ALSO TELL YOU APART FROM THEM.

HOW'S THIS?
HMM...

YOU SMELL A LITTLE DIFFERENT FROM THE OTHER MONSTERS.

......
!?

IT'S A SUBTLE IFFERENCE.
YEP!

REALLY?

......

AND ONLY COME CLOSE WHEN IT'S YOU.
Y-YEAH, BUT...

SO I CAN AVOID THE OTHER ONES.
G... GOOD.

ARE YOU SURE?

OF COURSE!
I MIGHT BE THE ONLY PERSON IN THE WORLD WHO CAN!

YEAH... UM... HMM...

HEH HEH... THAT'S WHAT YOU GET FOR TRYING TO GET ME TO BELIEVE THAT NONSENSE.

SHE CAN SENSE ME... SENSE MIGI?

WAYS MIGI IS DIFFERENT FROM THE OTHER PARASITES:
• DIDN'T TAKE THE BRAIN, CAN'T CONTROL THE BODY
• DOESN'T WANT TO EAT PEOPLE
• SLEEPS FOR FOUR HOURS EVERYDAY.

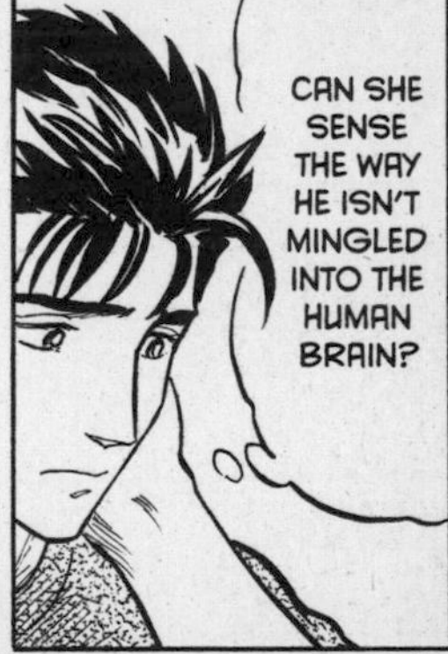

CAN SHE SENSE THE WAY HE ISN'T MINGLED INTO THE HUMAN BRAIN?

NO, SHE MUST BE LYING.

ARGH!
JUST MADE HINGS ORSE!

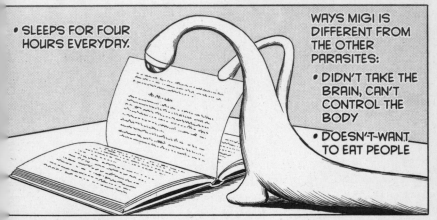

NOTHING AT ALL!
OH, NOTH-ING...

IS SOME-THING WRONG, SHINICHI?

ANOTHER ONE...

AND HE'S THE FOURTH ONE. THERE CAN'T BE THAT MANY OF THEM.

BUT HOW CAN HE BE A MONSTER?

BUT I DON'T GET IT. THERE MUST BE SOME WAY TO TELL SHINICHI APART.

NO...
I'LL JUST HAVE TO LEARN THE DIFFERENCE.

IS THAT MOVIE ANY GOOD? NO-BODY'S TALKING ABOUT IT.
IT'S A TEAR-JERKER.

MY FRIENDS ALL SAY THEY CRIED.
I'D PREFER SOMETHING A LITTLE MORE ESCAPIST...

BUT TOMORROW AT TEN?
SURE.

MONSTERS, MY ASS. HE WAS MAKING THAT UP!
WITHOUT A THOUGHT FOR MY FEELINGS.

DESTINY...
FATE, BINDING US TOGETHER...

THIS IS SOMETHING ELSE, LIKE...

SOMETHING ONLY I CAN...

LOOK AT ME.

COME ON... LOOK.

DOES THAT GIRL HAVE ANY POWERS?

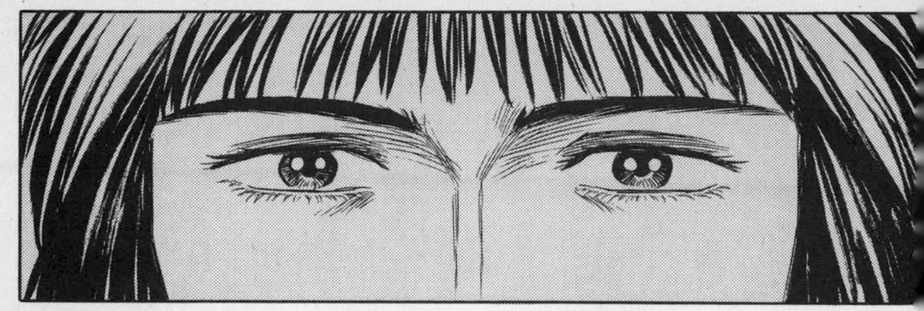

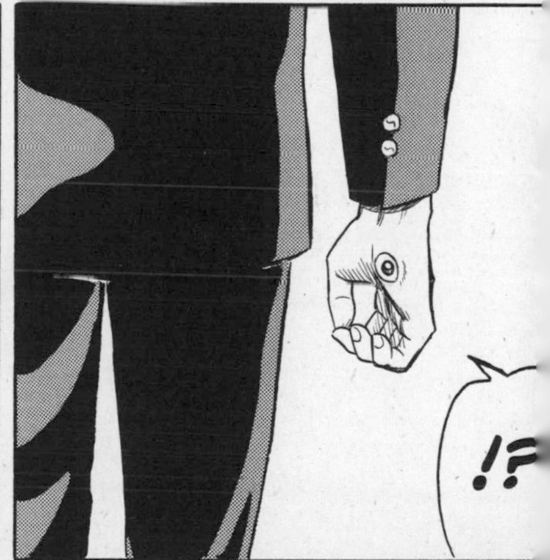

HAHH...
MY BACK HURTS...

MMM MMM!
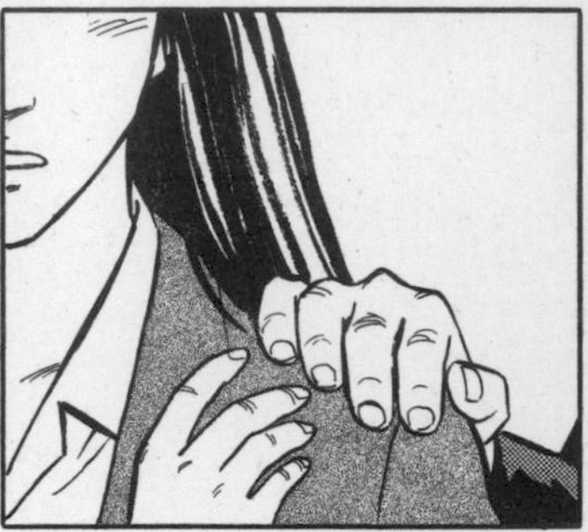

YIKES!

OH... MITSUO...

DON'T SNEAK UP ON ME! HOW LONG WERE YOU THERE?

WHAT ARE YOU DOING?

I WAS WATCHING YOU, AND YOU'RE ACTING REALLY STRANGE.
IT'S KIND OF PATHETIC.
P-PATHETIC?

S-SPEAK FOR YOURSELF STALKING ME...!
BE A MAN, YOU SPINELESS WIMP!

HE'S ALREADY GOT A GIRL-FRIEND. AND... HE WAS NEVER MEANT FOR YOU.

OH? THEN WHAT? I WAS MEAN FOR YOU HA! GET OVER YOURSELF

YOU MAY BE BIG, BUT INSIDE YOU'RE NOTHING! DON'T EVER SPEAK TO ME OR SHOW YOUR FACE BEFORE ME AGAIN!

HARSH. IT'S HARD TO...
TO HEAR SOMEONE YOU LO... LIKE REJECT YOU.

AH...

......

SORRY... BUT...
CAN'T
ELP IT.

I GOT CARRIED AWAY. SORRY.

RIGHT.
MMM?

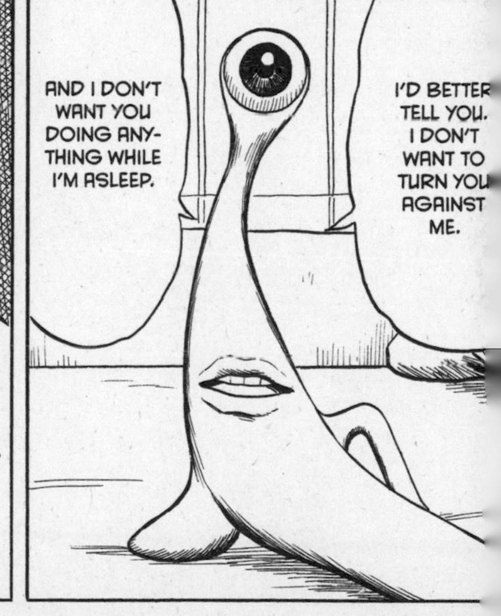
I'D BETTER TELL YOU. I DON'T WANT TO TURN YOU AGAINST ME.
AND I DON'T WANT YOU DOING ANY-THING WHILE I'M ASLEEP.

WHAT?

THAT GIRL, KANA...HER POWER'S GETTING STRONGER.
SHE'S SENDING OUT SIGNALS NOW.
SIGNALS?

THE SIGNALS PARASITES USE TO DETECT EACH OTHER'S LOCATION. ON THE WAY HOME FROM SCHOOL TODAY, *I SENSED HER.*

BUT...
BUT THAT EANS...

SHE CAN ONLY PUT OUT SIGNALS WHEN SHE'S CONCENTRATING REALLY HARD. NOT LIKE SHE'S DOING IT 24/7. AND THE RANGE IS VERY SMALL.

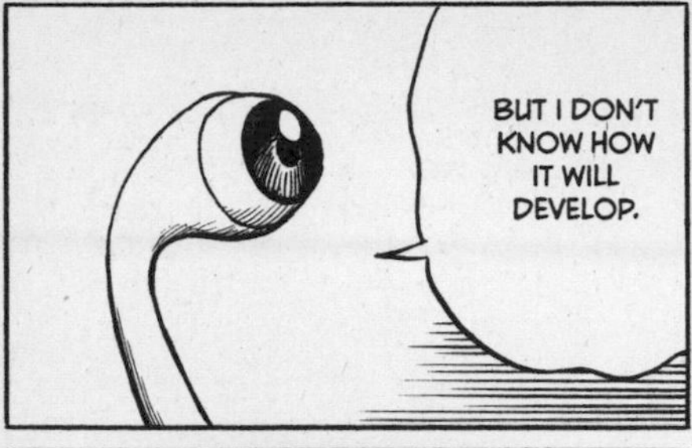
BUT I DON'T KNOW HOW IT WILL DEVELOP.

OH GOD...
OH GOD...

WHY DIDN'T YOU TELL ME SOONER!?

NO... THANKS FOR TELLING ME.

......

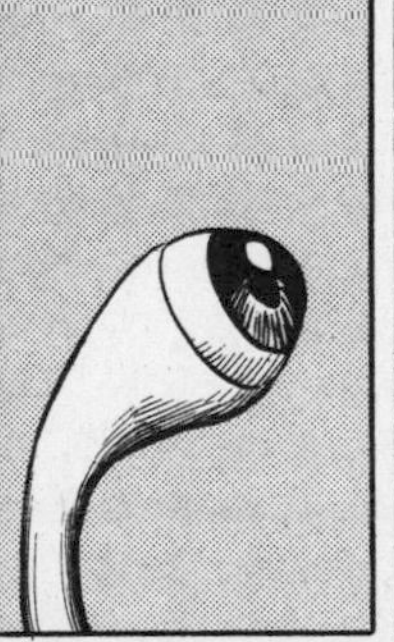

UM...

MIGI! I TOLD HER EVERYTHING, WHILE YOU WERE ASLEEP. ABOUT THE PARASITES, AND ABOUT YOU.

BUT...SHE DIDN'T BELIEVE ME.

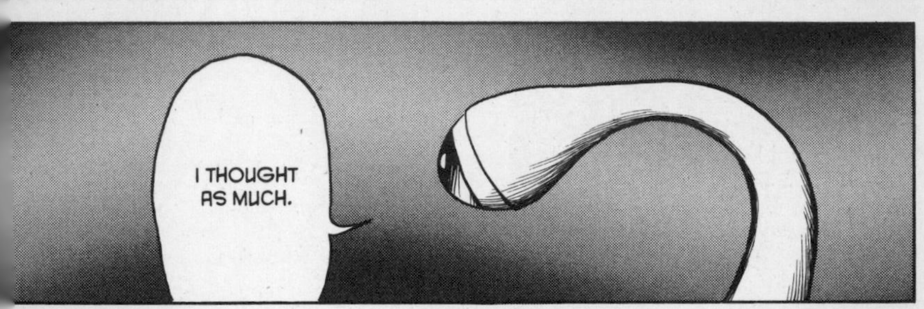

I THOUGHT AS MUCH.

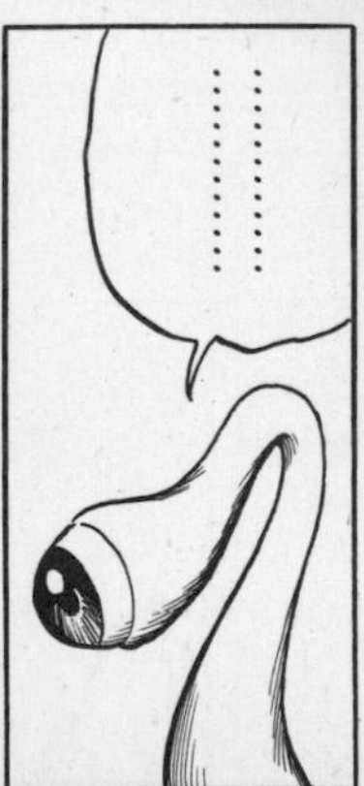

......

SHE'S NOT YOUR ENEMY. IF WE TELL HER... IF WE EXPLAIN, THEN SHE'LL KNOW WHAT HER POWER IS.

I WANT TO SHOW YO
TO HER.
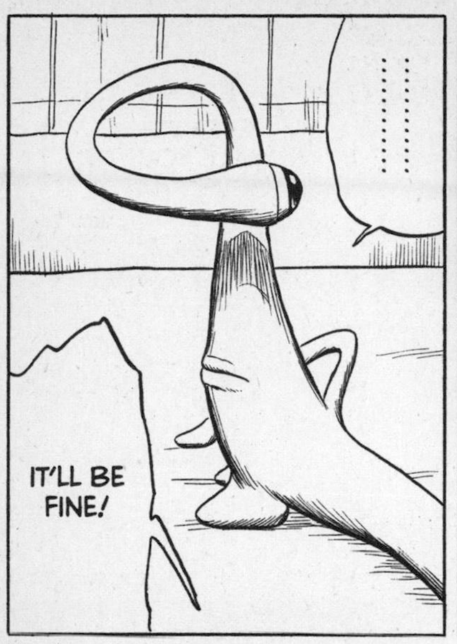
......
IT'LL BE FINE!

SO, UM...

IF SHE DOES TELL ANYONE, WE CAN LET THEM CHECK YOU OUT.
AS LONG AS YOU ACT LIKE A NORMAL HAND...

I MEAN, SHE'S JUST A HIGH SCHOOL GIRL.
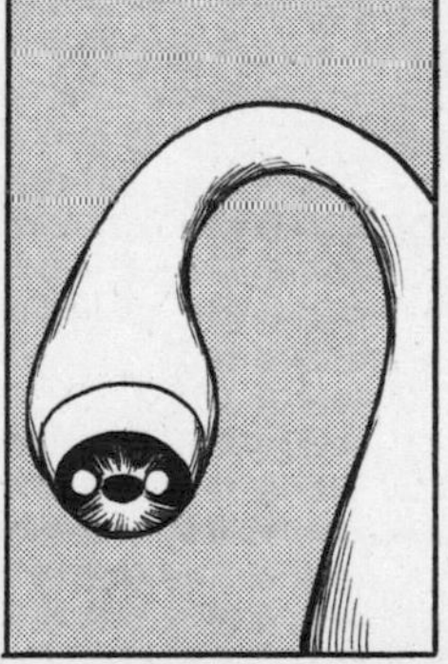

SO...!?

OKAY.

IF ONE OF THE ARASITES PICKS UP HER SIGNAL, SHE'LL BE DONE FOR!
GOT TO HURRY!

GREAT!

BUT OMORROW...

THEN, TOMOR-ROW...
STILL NOT HOME AT THIS HOUR? JESUS...

......

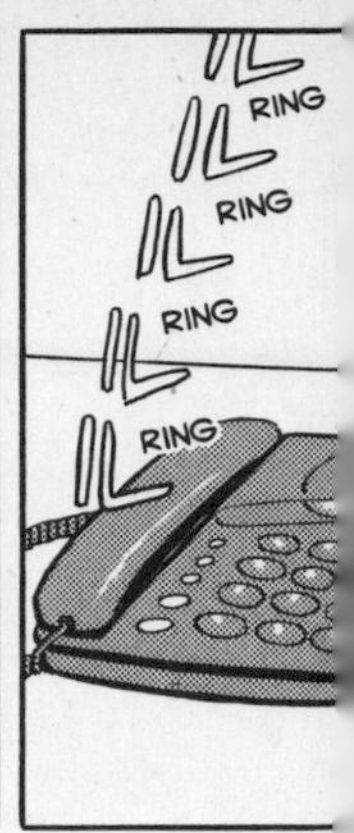
RING
RING
RING
RING

HELLO? MURANO SPEAKING... OH, IZUMI-KUN?

SORRY.
SOME-THING'S COME UP.

OH... OKAY THEN.
TOO BAD. SOME OTHER TIME?

YEAH... AND... SORRY.

CLICK

Shinichi

Shinichi
Ka

VROOOM.

OH, KANA! LONG TIME NO SEE!
MMM? NO MITSUO?

YEAH...
Shin
K

THE NEXT DAY
(SUNDAY)

SUNDAY...

YAWN!
MMM..

RING RING RING RING

I WANT TO MAKE THEM STRONGER...
GUESS I'LL GO TO THE PARK, HON MY POWERS

AH, MORE OF THE SAME?

IT'S URGENT.
THIS TIME I HAVE PROOF!

HE NEVER LEARNS...
OKAY, I GUESS.

OKAY, MIGI?
EH?

I'M NEAR THE STATION, SO IF WE COULD MEET...

MMM?
TAP TAP

THREE PARASITES COMING TOWARD US BY CAR.
URP
STRAIGHT AT US.

AH! SORRY! IGNORE THAT! I'LL CALL YOU BACK.

OH, WAIT!

I WILL CALL BACK, SO DON'T GO OUTSIDE! PLEASE!

WHAT THE... BUT HE'S CLOSE BY?

VROOOM
キキッ
THAT CAR!

CLUNK

DAMN IT!
SCREECH
WAIT, SHINICHI!

THEY KNOW WE'RE HERE.
IF WE MOVE, THEY'LL SUSPECT US!

PRETEND YOU'RE ON THE PHONE!

RIGHT...I'LL SHOW HIM MY POWER.

THAT I CAN SENSE YOU...AND NO ONE ELSE CAN...
THAT I CAN DO SOMETHING THAT MURANO GIRL CAN'T...

AND THAT WAY YOU..

...WILL FALL FOR ME.

ブオオオー
VROOOM

THIS IS SO

BUT NOT PARTICULARLY UNUSUAL.
IT'S NOT LIKE THEY CAN TELL YOUR BRAIN IS INTACT.

LOOKS LIKE THEY'RE INCREASING... BETTER GET THIS OVER WITH.
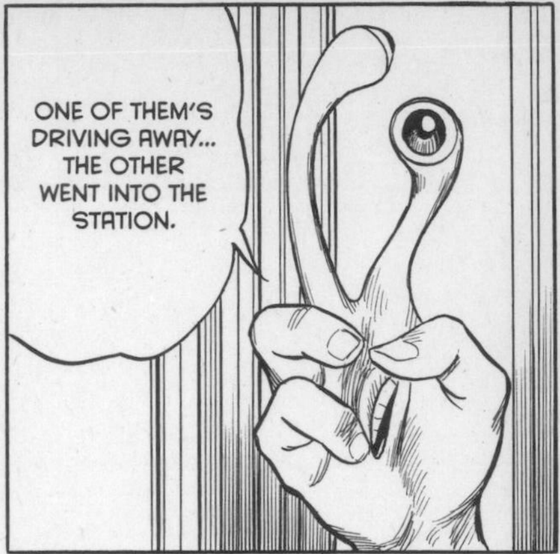
ONE OF THEM'S DRIVING AWAY... THE OTHER WENT INTO THE STATION.

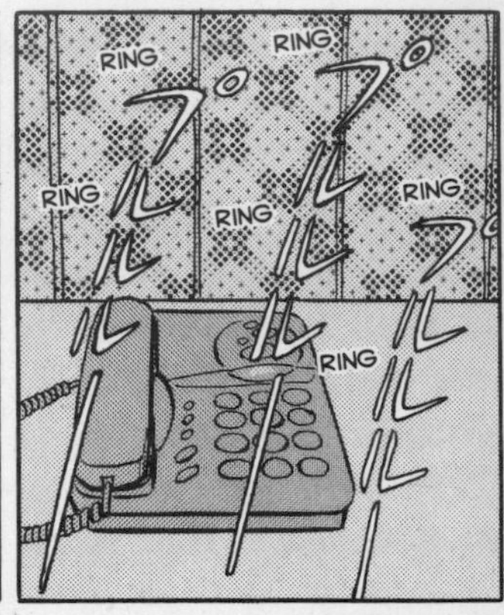
RING
RING
RING
RING
RING
RING

YOU'VE GOT TO BE KIDDING ME!

CHAPTER 31: RED TEARS

I THINK I KNOW WHICH WAY HER HOUSE IS, BUT...
IS SHE HEADED THIS WAY?
CREAK

I TOLD HER NOT TO GO ANY-WHERE!

SHE WAS LYING, RIGHT?

KANA SAID THAT?
SHE CAN DISTINGUISH ME FROM THE OTHERS?

I KNEW IT!

IT'S HARD TO BELIEVE. EVEN WE HAVE TROUBLE TELLING EACH OTHER APART, AND FOR A HUMAN...

WHAT NOW? DO WE HEAD TOWARD HER PLACE?
BUT IF I MISS HER...

BUT I DID TELL HER I WAS NEAR THE STATION...

I'D BETTER CALL AGAIN.
SQUEAK

BUT WHAT IF SHE WENT OUT FOR SOMETHING ELSE? IN THA CASE...

IS IT SHINICHI?
GOT ONE!

!

IT'S A BIT TOO FAR FROM THE STATION, BUT...

I REALLY SHOULD HAVE FOUND OUT WHERE SHE LIVED...

NO GOOD. WE HAVE TO HEAD FOR HER HOME.
CHUNK

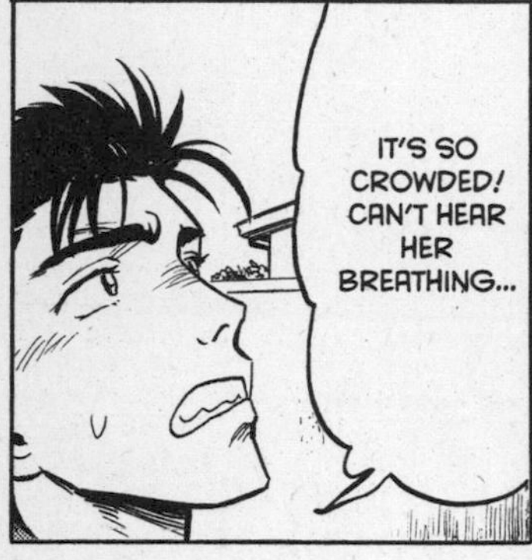
IT'S SO CROWDED! CAN'T HEAR HER BREATHING...

MIGI, YOU CAN'T SENSE HER SIGNAL ANYWHERE?

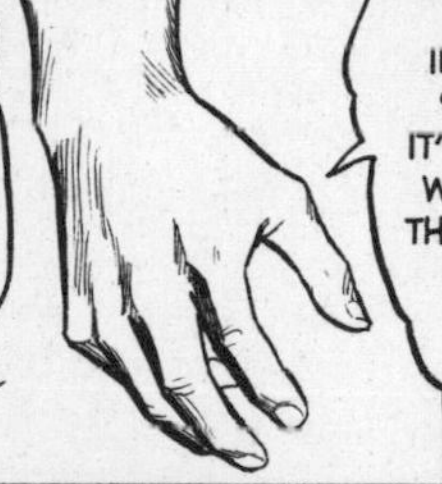
IMPOS-SIBLE. IT'S MUCH WEAKER THAN OUR OWN.

AND SHE MIGHT NOT EVEN BE EMITTING IT NOW.

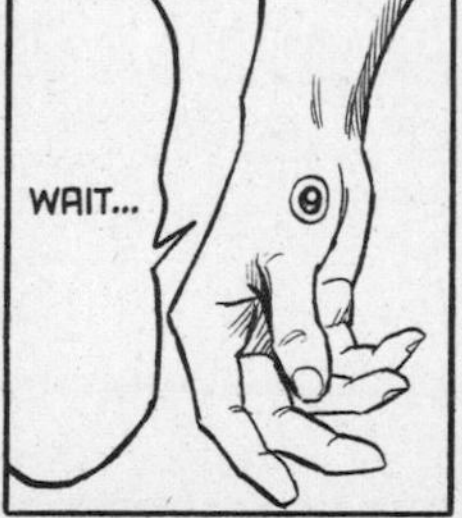
WAIT...

YOU FOUND HER?

NO. A PARASITE.

WHERE....?

JUST A LITTLE OFF THE DIRECTION WE'RE HEADED...

BUT SHE MIGHT HAVE CAUGHT THAT SIGNAL FIRST.
WHERE?

LEFT HERE.

WAIT, I'VE BEEN HERE...

AH HA HA HA!
WHAT DO YOU KNOW?
SAME PLACE AS LAST TIME!
HE DID THIS DELIBERATELY.
IS HE TESTING MY POWER?

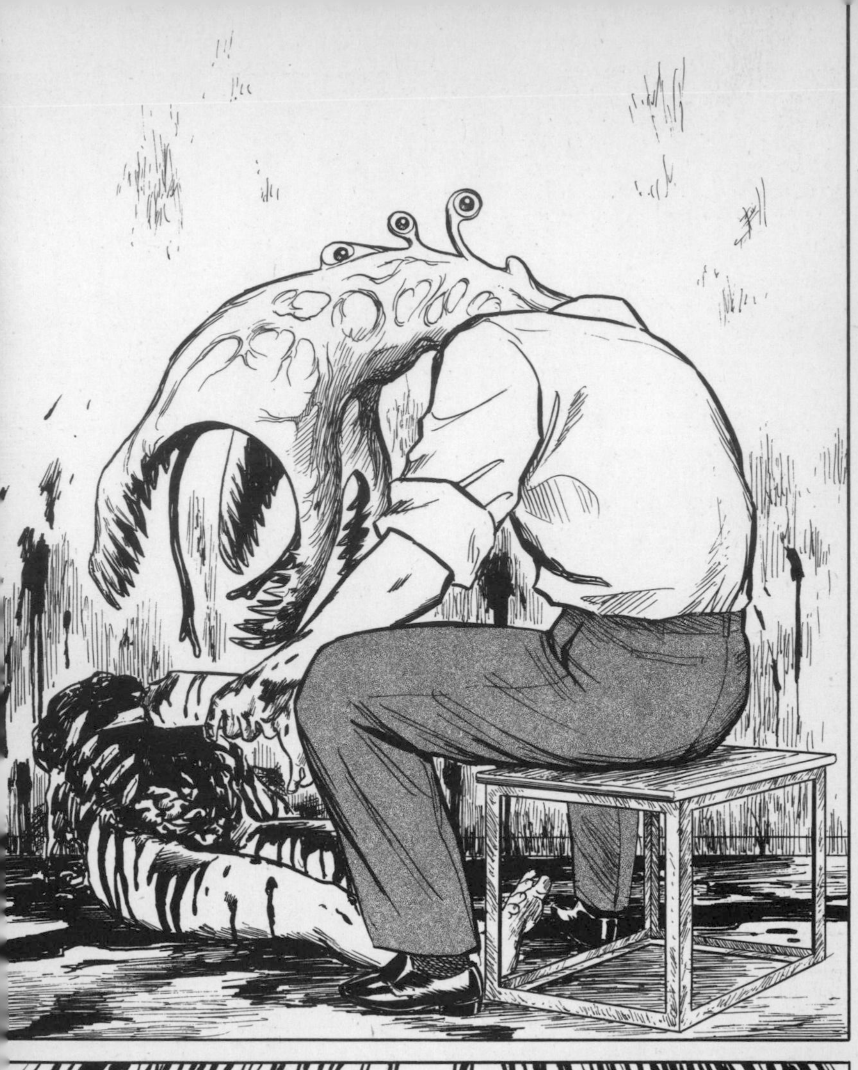

!?
A HUMAN?
I THOUGHT THE SIGNAL WAS WEAK...
AKI
SWISH

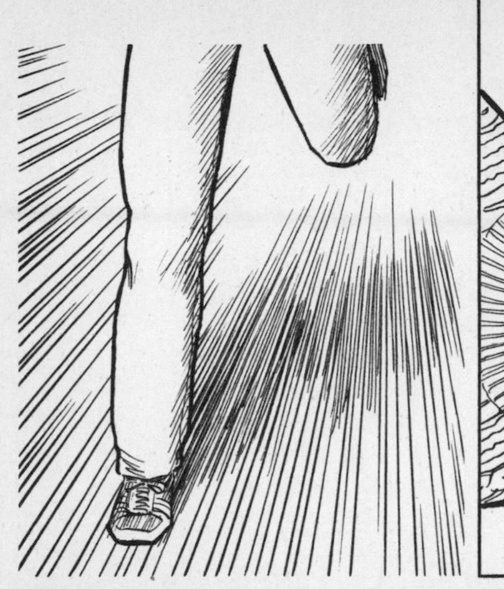

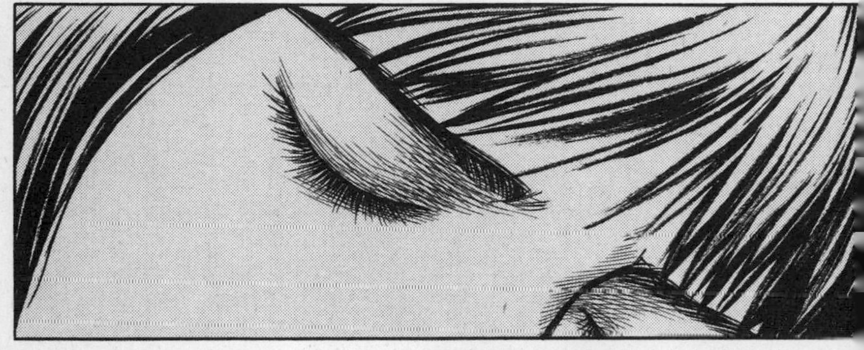

WHOOSH

OVE

OH, GOD...
WHY?

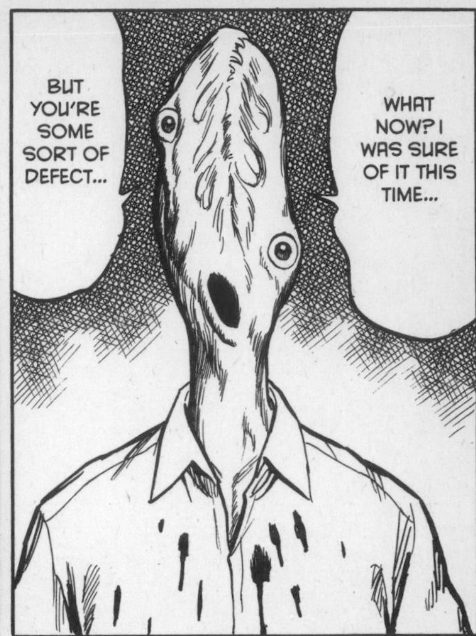
WHAT NOW? I WAS SURE OF IT THIS TIME...
BUT YOU'RE SOME SORT OF DEFECT...

MIGI...

PROTECT ME.

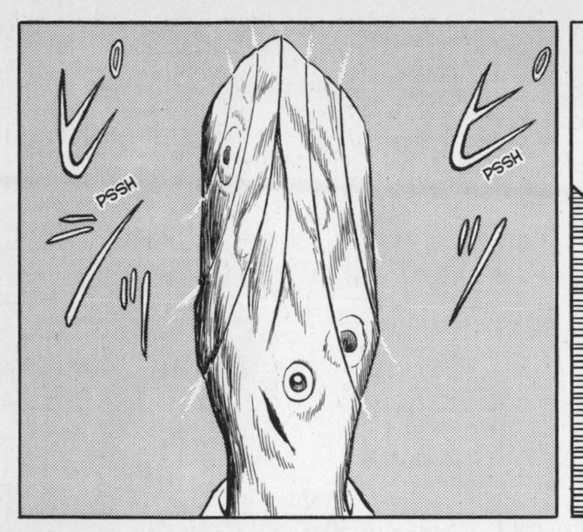
PSSH
PSSH

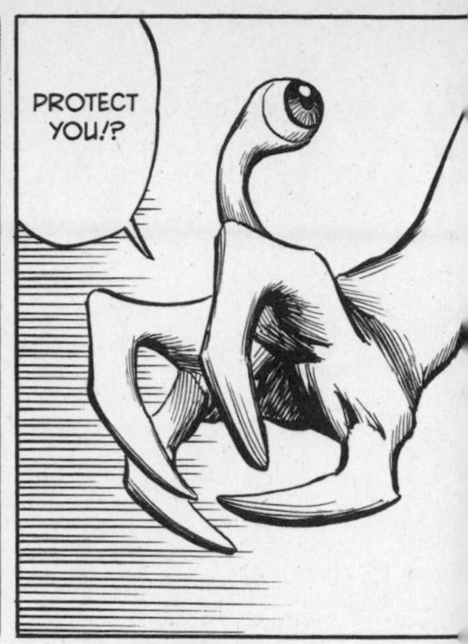
PROTECT YOU!?

VVWIP!

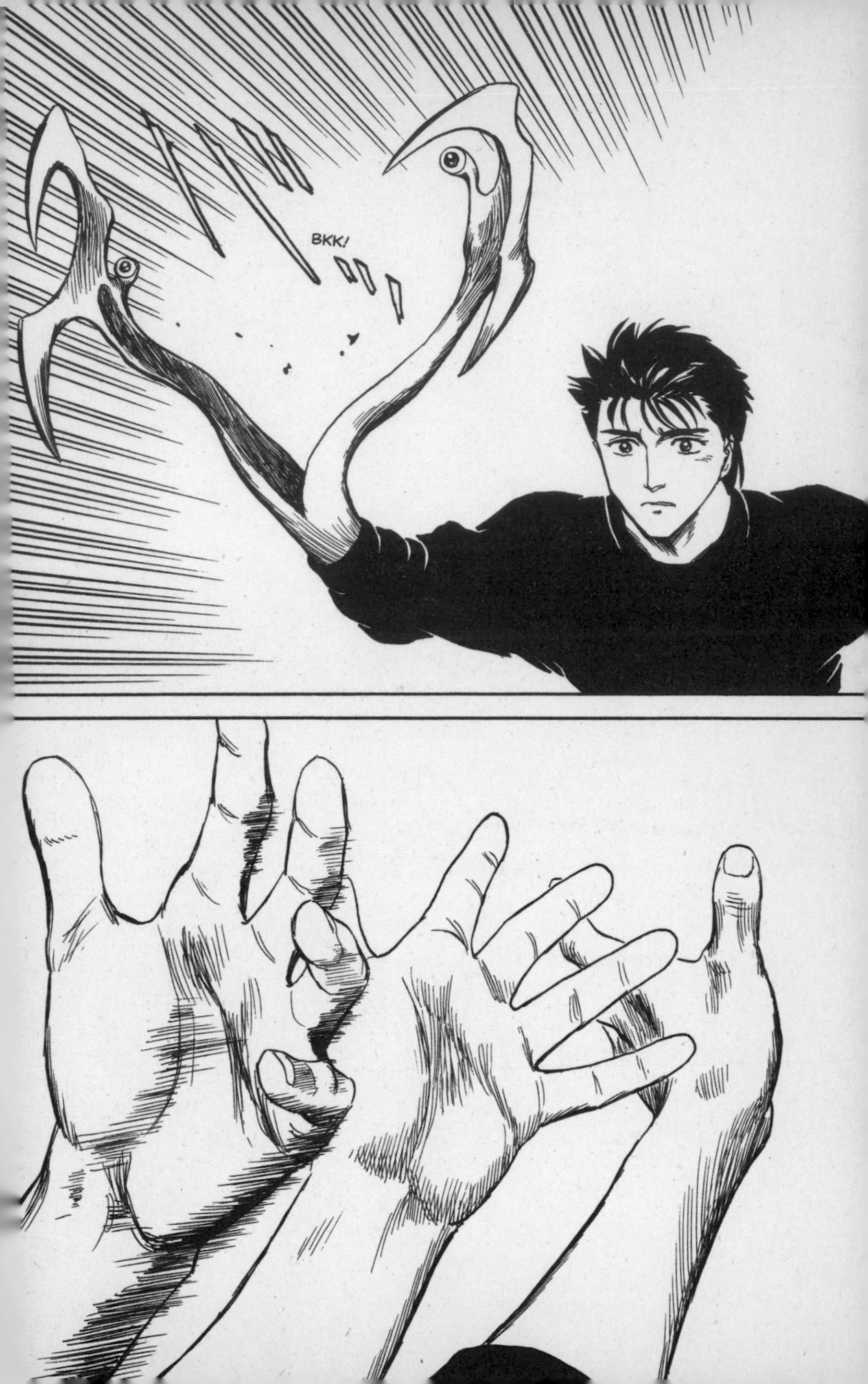
BKK!

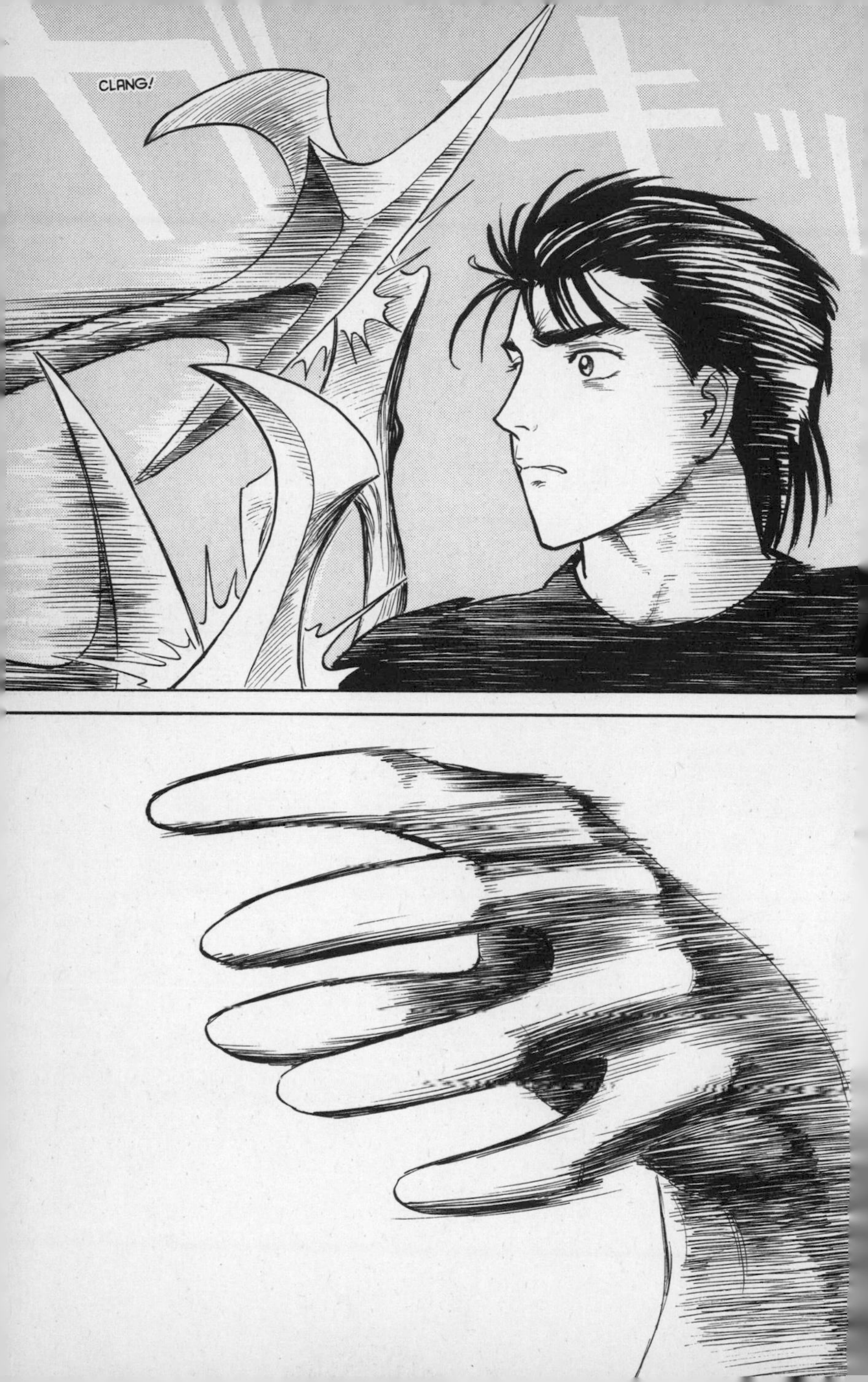

CLANG!

SPLAT!

ブ

THUD!

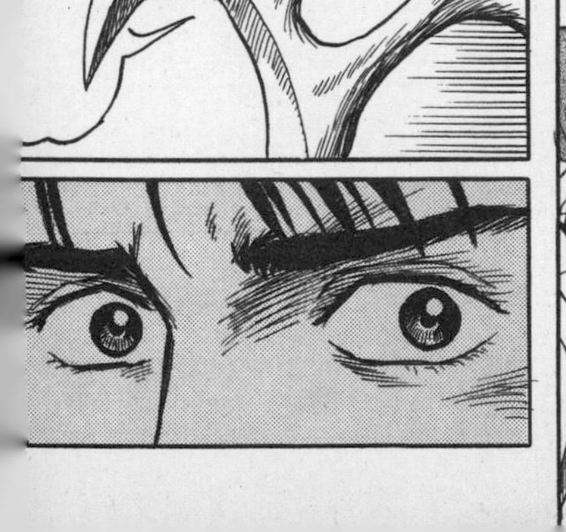

SPLAT

IT'S NO GOOD. SHE'S LOST TOO MUCH BLOOD.
OH NO...

UNH...

KANA!

MMM...

OH...

I KNEW YOU'D COME HERE... I COULD FEEL IT...

HANG ON!

THIS HAPPENED BEFORE...
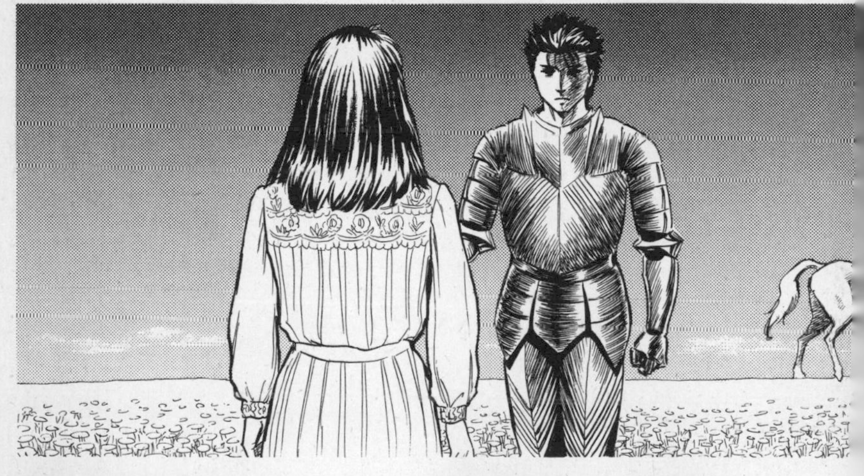

A DREAM...TOO EMBARRASSING TO TALK ABOUT...

......

HEY! KANA!! KA.....

Ka
Shinichi
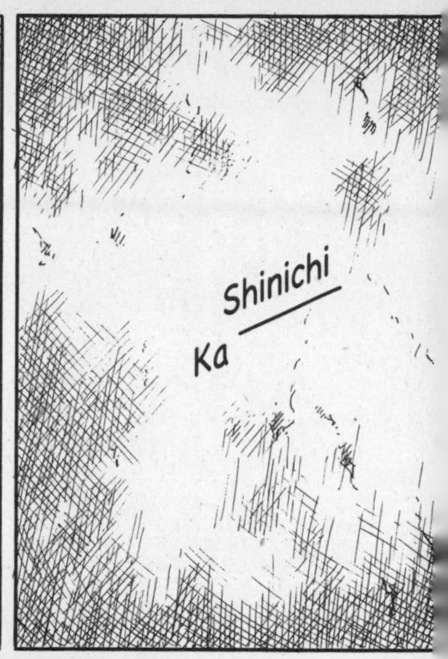
Ka
Shinichi

YET SOME PEOPLE ARE PLEASED TO HAVE ANOTHER SAMPLE...
SUCH A YOUNG VICTIM.

THAT BOY FOUND HER?

......

SOB...

REALLY!?
KEEP THIS SECRET: HIS MOTHER WAS KILLED, TOO.

SHH.
HE KNEW THE VICTIM? HE SEEMS AWFULLY CALM...

HE'S NOT FRIENDLY.
SICK OF TALKING TO US, I SUPPOSE.

AND WE MADE HIM GIVE US A HAIR, JUST IN CASE.
THAT WOULD DO IT.

BUT WHAT BUGS ME...
THE GIRL WAS KILLED BY A PARASITE, BUT WHAT KILLED THE PARASITE?

IT'S IMPOSSIBLE FOR ANY HUMAN TO DODGE THE TENTACLES, BREAK THROUGH THE RIBS...
...YANK OUT THE HEART AND THEN FLING THE BODY SO HARD IT BROKE THE WALL.
THERE MUST HAVE BEEN AT LEAST ONE OTHER PARASITE THERE.

THE MONSTERS ARE FIGHTING EACH OTHER?
WHAT ELSE CAN WE THINK?

BUT HE DIDN'T SEE ANYTHING, APPARENTLY.

EVERYTHING BLOWS UP IN MY FACE.
RUSTLE
IF I HADN'T CALLED HER THAT DAY...
IF I'D GONE TO SEE A MOVIE WITH MURANO...
RUSTLE

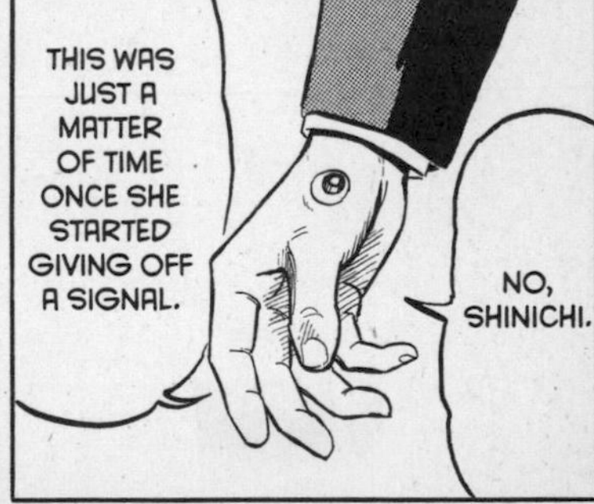
NO, SHINICHI.
THIS WAS JUST A MATTER OF TIME ONCE SHE STARTED GIVING OFF A SIGNAL.

YOU DID EVERYTHING YOU COULD. YOU HAVE NOTHING TO FEEL GUILTY ABOUT.
HA! DON'T TALK TO ME ABOUT...

RUSTLE
RUSTLE

HAHH HAHH...

IT'S AL YOUR FAULT.
IT'S ALL YOUR FAULT KANA.....!

WHACK!

WHY DIDN'T YOU PROTECT HER!?

SHE WAS...
ALREADY DEAD.

HOW CAN YOU LOOK SO CALM!?

THWACK!

WHOOMP!

DON'T YOU EVEN KNOW?
HOW SHE FELT ABOUT YOU?
THUNK!
BAM!
THUMP!

YOU AREN'T HUMAN!

NOT HUMAN...

YOU DON'T BLEED, YOU DON'T CRY...!!

WHOOSH

THUD!

YEAH!

WHUMP!
UNH!

THWACK!

WHAM!

UGH...

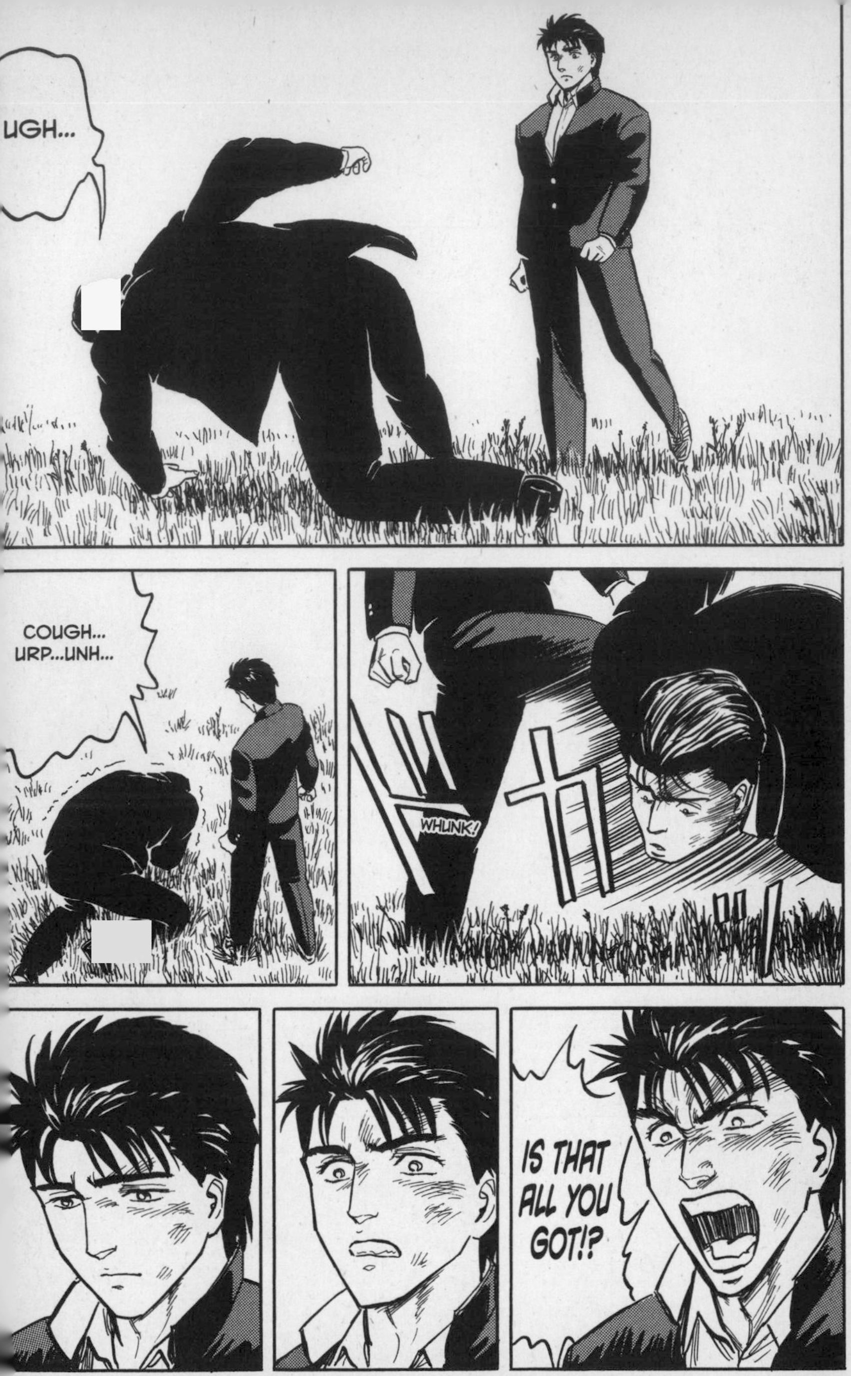

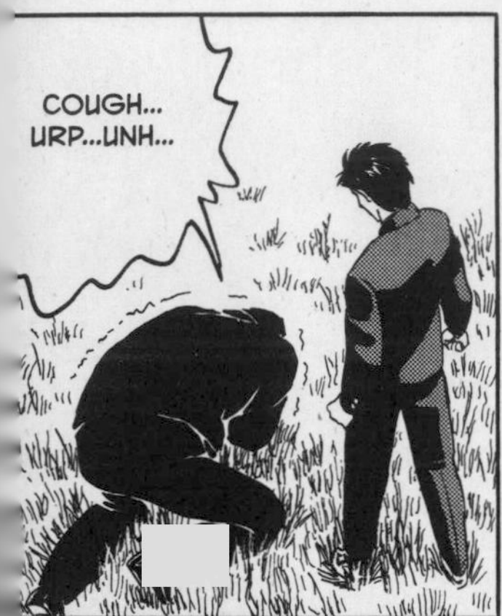
COUGH...
URP...UNH...

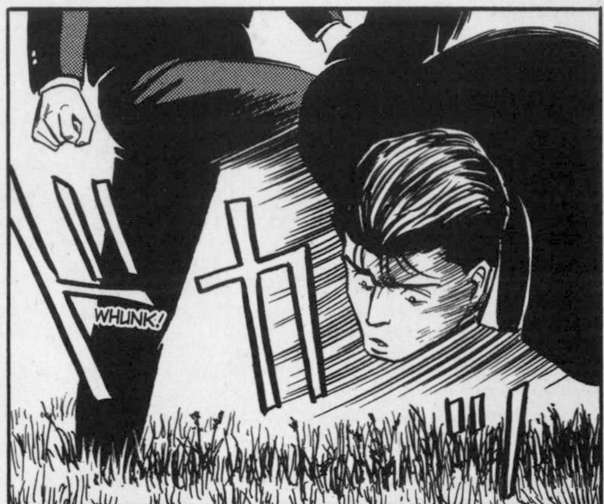
WHUNK!

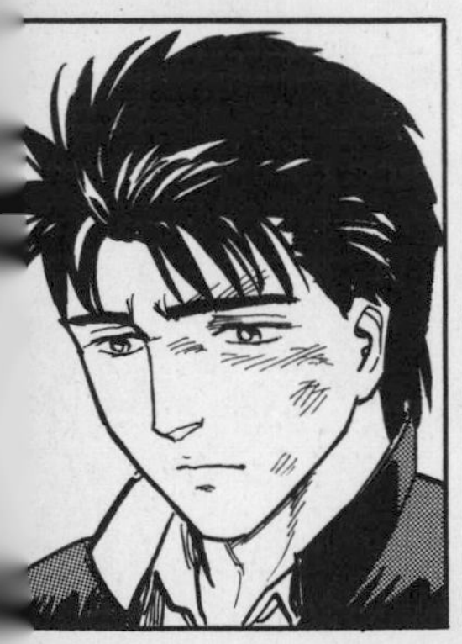

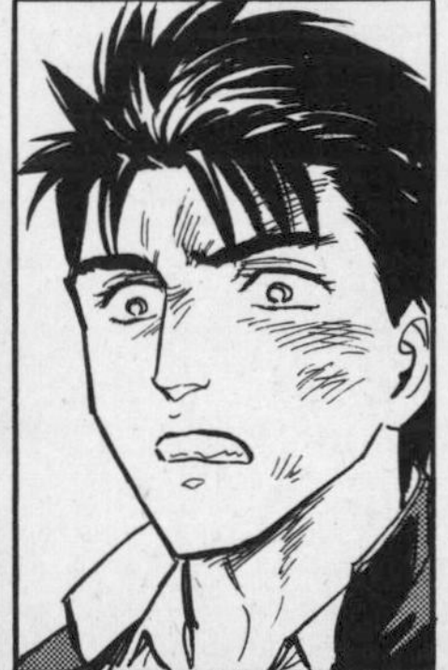

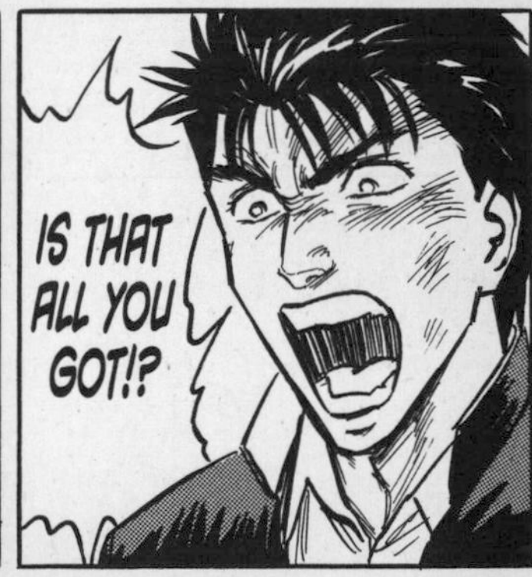
IS THAT ALL YOU GOT!?

UNH...

IF I DON'T HOLD BACK, I'LL PUT A HOLE THROUGH HIM, TOO.

WHY *AM* I FEELING SO CALM?
HEH HEH. GUESS I'M REALLY NOT HUMAN.

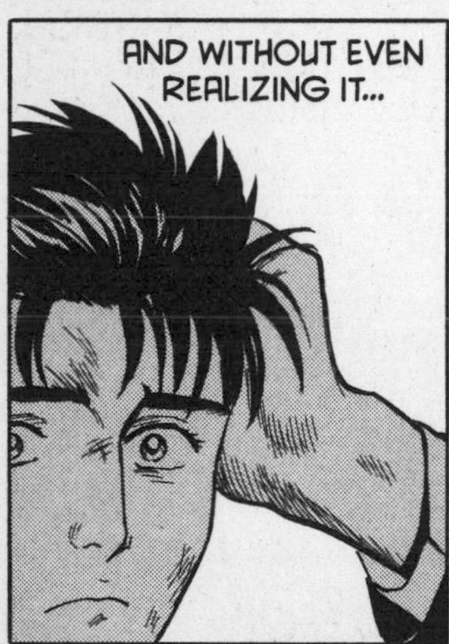
AND WITHOUT EVEN REALIZING IT...

WITHOUT MY EVER NOTICING...
HAS HE TAKEN OVER MY BRAIN?

SOMEONE I KNOW IS DEAD...
KANA IS DEAD...
BUT I CAN'T CRY.

THUNK!

WHAM!
WHAM!
WHAM!

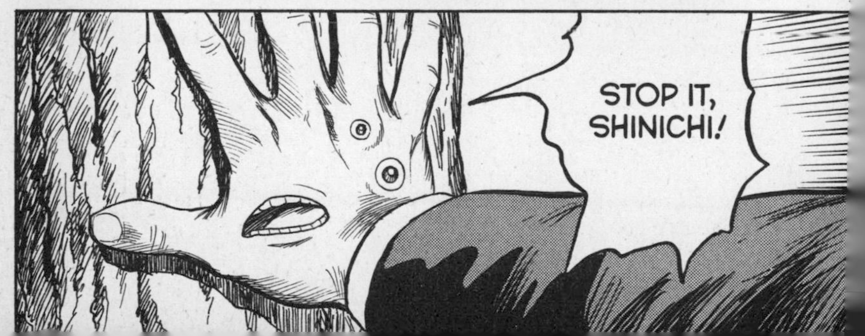
STOP IT, SHINICHI!

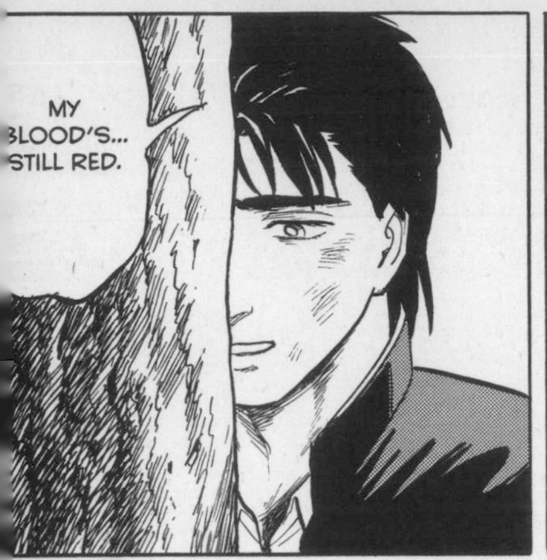
MY
BLOOD'S...
STILL RED.

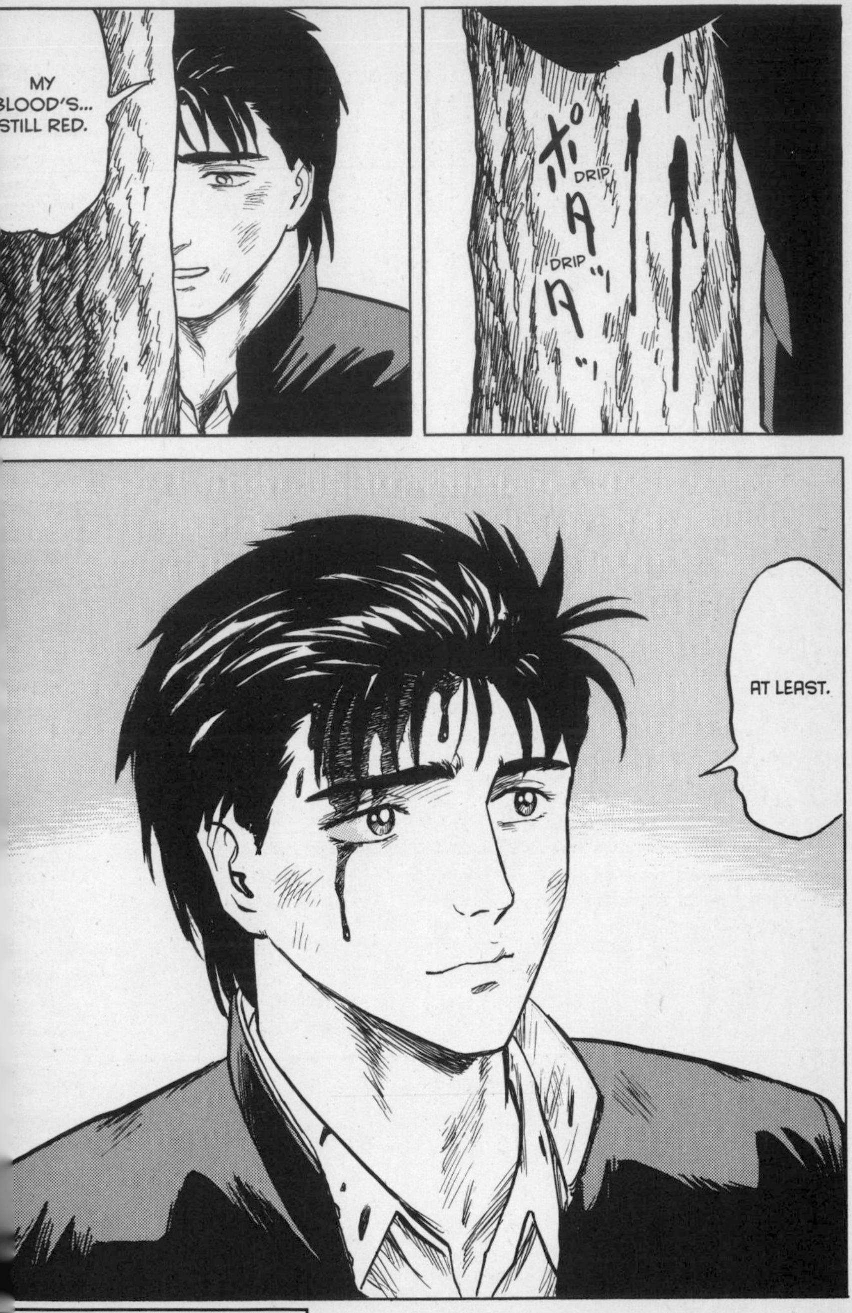

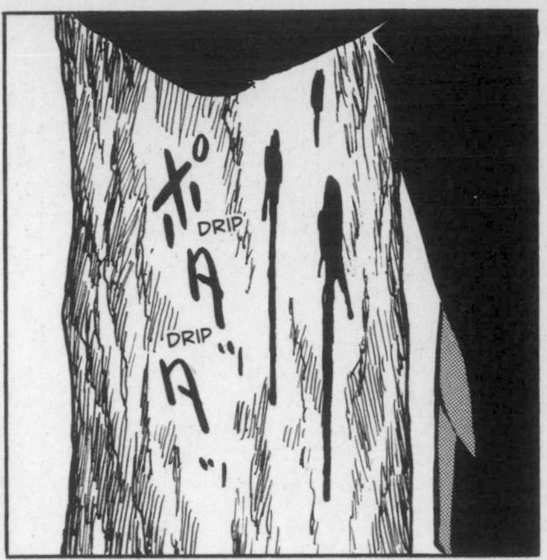
DRIP
DRIP

AT LEAST.

HAPTER 31: THE END

From the Monthly Afternoon Readers' page....

PARASYTE 4 vol. 9

"Can't they live together peacefully, like we do with livestock? I'm starting to be impressed by their struggles to stay alive."
(Kanagawa Prefecture, Taka, 30, Employee)

"Coexistance might be possible. After all, there are far fewer parasites than there are humans, so why not let them eat a few of us? Or so a nature-loving, reckless alien might say."
(Hitoshi Iwaaki)

(From *Afternoon*, July 1992)

"*Parasyte* is really scary. So is Shinichi. I hope he doesn't become any less human..."
(Niigata Prefecture, Moomin, 29)

"I believe the protagonist of a story is like a traveler in places ordinary humans seldom tread. As readers, I hope that you will follow him into this inhuman world. The further we get from human, the greater our understanding of what it is to be human may become. I hope!"
(Hitoshi Iwaaki)

(From *Afternoon*, November 1992)

THE READERS ASK THE AUTHOR ANSWERS

From the Monthly Afternoon Readers' page....

PARASYTE 4

vol. 10

THE READERS ASK, THE AUTHOR ANSWERS

"I'm getting really worried that this series will end soon. Please let the joy of reading this manga continue! It's so exciting, and you never know what will happen next! Trying to guess is one of my greatest pleasures."
(Hokkaido, Takei Chikako, 31, Housewife)

"Just as what's going to happen next is a closely guarded secret, so is the projected length of the book. It will eventually end. I think there are two ways for a long-running manga series to end—the story can die, or the story can conclude. For example, many of Tezuka Osamu's manga end in the latter fashion. I hope Parasyte can end that way, too."
(Hitoshi Iwaaki)

(From *Afternoon*, December 1992)

"Parasites kill and eat humans to survive. But this makes humans worse than them! We kill animals and plants for profit."
(Saga Prefecture, A.H., 16, Student)

"Humans, especially those in developed countries, are living extremely luxurious lives. But that luxury is linked to environmental damage. I think the feeling that humans are 'worse' comes from guilt at having averted our gaze from the chart showing that luxury leads to that destruction."
(Hitoshi Iwaaki)

(From *Afternoon*, May 1993)

HERE, AND HERE...
HERE.
HERE
HERE
HERE
HERE AND HERE
IF WE CHART THEM, WE CAN SEE THAT THERE ARE ALREADY QUITE A NUMBER OF "DINING ROOMS."

PERSONALLY, I THINK THERE COULD BE FEWER...

CHAPTER 32: TAMURA REIKO

DOESN'T THAT SUGGEST THE NUMBER IS INADEQUATE?
AND THAT ABANDONED BUILDING WHERE ONE OF US WAS KILLED THE OTHER DAY...THAT WASN'T ONE OF THE DESIGNATED AREAS.

I AGREE. THERE ARE TOO MANY.

THIS ISN'T THAT SIMPLE.

IT HAD NOTHING TO DO WITH IT. HE WAS SIMPLY SELFISH. HE FORGOT OUR COMMON PURPOSE, AND SIMPLY FOLLOWED HIS STOMACH LIKE A COMMON DOG OR CAT. WE'RE BETTER OFF WITHOUT HIM.

AND STILL THE KILLER HAS NOT APPEARED.
THE HUMANS HAVE OBTAINED ANOTHER SAMPLE.

"SHIMADA HIDEO" AND I WERE INVESTIGATIN HIM.

WELCOME BACK, "TAMURA-SAN."

HOW ARE YOU, "GOTO-SAN"?

PERFECTLY FINE.

I'M CERTAIN HE'S THE ONE THAT KILLED OUR KIND IN THE ABANDONED BUILDING.
PRESUMABLY, HE SAW HIS FRIEND KILLED, AND GREW EMOTIONAL.

YES. THE BRAIN SURVIVED, AND IS COHABITING WITH THE PARASITE.

HIS FRIEND? EMOTIONAL? YOU MEAN HIS BRAIN IS COMPLETELY HUMAN?

HE IS NOT THAT DANGEROUS. HE IS MORE VALUABLE AS A SPECIMEN.

SHOULDN'T WE SIMPLY KILL HIM?

I COULDN'T SAY.
BUT I WILL ASK THAT YOU LEAVE HIM IN MY HANDS.

THIS BOY... DID HE HAVE ANYTHING TO DO WITH "SHIMADA HIDEO'S" SPECTACULAR LAST STAND? IF HE DID, THEN THIS IS HIS SECOND TIME.

I'M AWARE THAT YOU LOVE YOUR RESEARCH, "TAMURA-SAN," BUT PLEASE TRY TO AVOID ANYTHING DANGEROUS.

......

I AM WORKING...

FOR THE FUTURE POTENTIAL OF ALL OF US.

HMM...THEN WE WILL LEAVE THIS BOY TO YOU.

OH, AND "TAMURA-SAN..."
HOW IS YOUR CHILD?

ALIVE. IN THE USUAL FASHIO
BUT I WILL HAVE TO GET HELP FROM HUMANS IN RAISING IT.

OH?

うぎゃああ
WAAAAA!
ぎゃああ
WAAAAAH!

NOW, NOW...
WHAT'S WRONG? IT'S NOT YOUR DIAPER...
WAAAAAH

CLICK.
OH, MOMMY'S HERE...

WELCOME HOME.
WAAAAAAAH!

WAAAAH!
HE HAS QUITE A VOICE.

AAAAAAAAAH!
MM!?

WAAAAAAAH
UM, WELL, I'D BETTER...
WAAAAH

?

ふぎゃあああ

WAAAAAAAAAAAAH

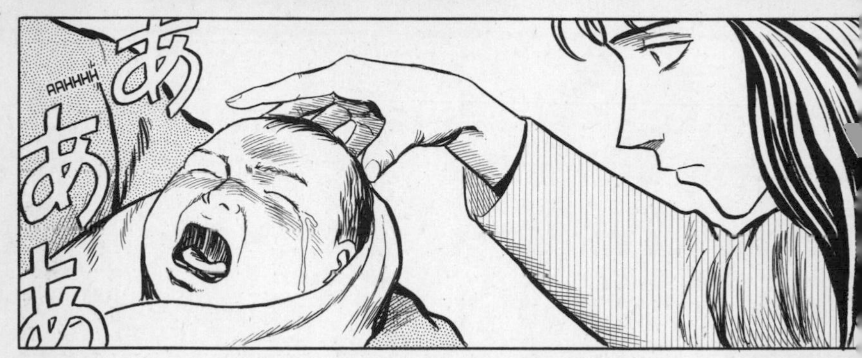

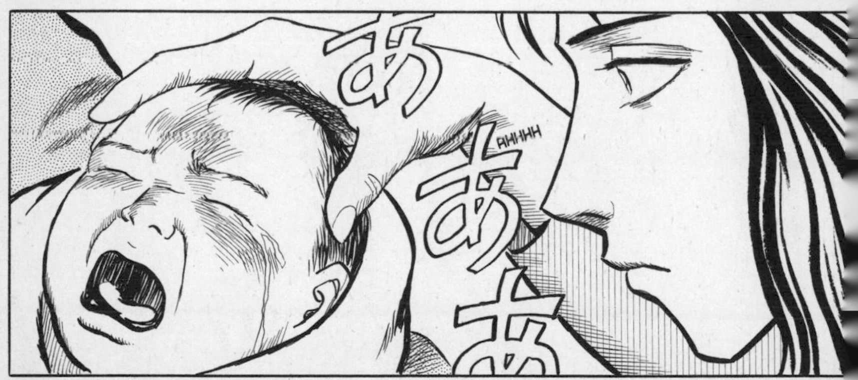

SHUSH.

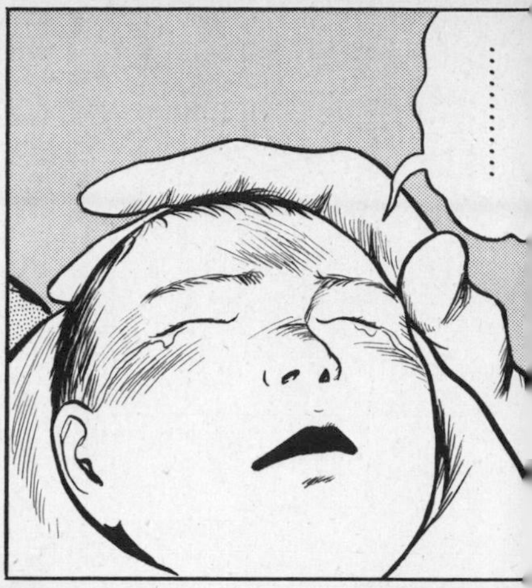

THANK YOU. I'LL SEE YOU AGAIN TOMORROW.
Y- YES...

IS SHE REALLY A MOTHER?

BUT IT DID STOP CRYING.

I HAVE IT TRAINED WELL, DON'T I?

EH.. AH...

EXCUSE ME!

......
SLAM

RATTLE

I'LL LET IT GROW A LITTLE MORE BEFORE STARTING TO EXPERIMENT.

AS FOR THE BOY...
I THINK I'LL GET HUMAN HELP THERE.

EH!? SERIOUSLY!?

BOW

SAY, IZUMI...

THE OTHER DAY...
THAT GIRL FROM NORTH HIGH WAS KILLED...

YOU FOUND THE BODY?

UM, I HEARD...

SLAM

WHAT WAS IT LIKE?

CHEER UP!
SLAP
ポン

......

YOU AREN'T HUMAN!!

SHALL WE?

YOU
OKAY?

YEAH...
YOU?

I'M FINE.

THE OTHER DAY...WHEN WE WERE SUPPOSED TO SEE THAT MOVIE, I...

......
......

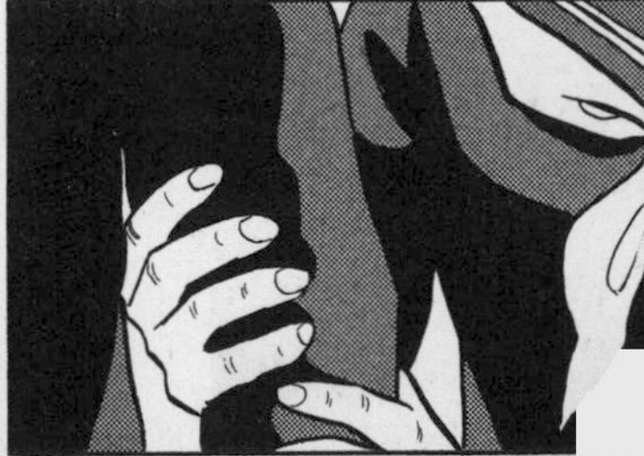

I THOUGHT IT WOULD BE HARD TO TELL HER ABOUT KANA'S DEATH...

EVERYTHING I THINK TO SAY IS TERRIFYING.

GOT A
GIRLFRIEND?
LUCKY...

IZUMI

THREE DAYS NOW. NOTHING UNUSUAL SO FAR.
IT'S BEEN PRETTY DULL...

YEAH, I CAN KEEP DIGGING. SURE.

YEAH, THAT'S RIGHT...HIS MOTHER'S DISAPPEAR-ANCE IS THE ONLY THING.
I'LL NEED TO CHECK INTO THAT A LITTLE LONGER, BUT THE BOY HIM-SELF IS JUST AN ORDINARY HIGH SCHOOL KID.

CLICK.
カタ

ORDINARY HIGH SCHOOL KID?
HUMANS ARE NOT VERY OBSERVANT.

BUT THERE ARE THINGS ONLY HUMANS CAN DO... THINGS "SHIMADA HIDEO" COULDN'T.

LET ME TRY SOME-THING.

HA
HA
HA.
FOUR IS ALMOST TOO MANY!
IF HE'S ANY-THING LIKE THIS PICTURE, YOU'D HAVE TO HOLD BACK FOR FEAR OF KILLING HIM.

ANYTHING IS FINE?

THERE!
THE KID IN THE PICTURE.

I SHOULD HAVE TAKEN THIS ALONE...
TOUGH.

ONE HUNDRED THOUSAND TO KICK HIS ASS?

UM...DO I KNOW YOU?

HOLD ON! I DON'T...

WOAH!
SWING

SWISH
REMEMBER...
HEY!

OH!
OH!
STAND STILL!

SWISH
SWISH
SWISH
YOU...
LITTLE...

STOP IT!

SWING

WOAH, WAIT!

GRAB

CLUNK

SWING

THUNK

EH...

THUNK

NOW THAT'S
WHAT I CALL
A SURPRISE...

SO,
UM...
EEEEK!

EEEEK?

WHO PUT YOU UP TO THIS?
SOME WOMAN... NEVER SEEN HER BEFORE...

HEY!
WHY'D YOU DO IT?

HUNH?

DID YOU NOTICE ANYTHING ELSE?

APPEARANCE CAN BE DECEIVING.

I'VE NEVER SEEN ANYONE MOVE SO FAST! LIKE THE WIND!
TINK
TINK

I MEAN, ANYTHING UNNATURAL FOR A HUMAN...

FOR EXAMPLE, THE WAY HIS RIGHT HAND MOVED?

NOT REALLY?

JUST AS I THOUGHT...
SOME-THING ELSE HAS CHANGED...

CHAPTER 33: WITNESS

IZUMI SHINICHI, 17, HIGH SCHOOL JUNIOR. AT FIRST I THOUGHT HE WAS PERFECTLY ORDINARY, BUT...
THE MORE I INVESTIGATED, THE MORE I REALIZED JUST HOW WRONG I'D BEEN.

わははははは
HA HA HA HA HA HA HA

YOUR GIRLFRIEND'S RIGHT BEHIND US.

AH...

SATOMI, I HATE TO SAY IT, BUT...

DON'T BE SO SHEEPISH!

THAT'S NOT ALL. THEY SAY HE KNEW THE DEAD GIRL.

YOU'VE HEARD ABOUT IZUMI, RIGHT? THAT HE FOUND THAT DEAD GIRL...

THE OTHER DAY...WHEN WE WERE SUPPOSED TO SEE THAT MOVIE, I...

I KNOW

YOU'VE BEEN GOING OUT WITH HER A WHILE, RIGHT?

SO? ONCE A WEEK?

ONCE A...?

NO! WE HAVEN'T...!

NO WAY! YOU SERIOUSLY HAVEN'T DONE HER YET?

SHHH!
DON'T YELL!

ギャハハハハ
HA HA HA HA HA
SHUT UP.
JUST DO IT, MAN!
THEY'RE HAVING FUN...

....

ONLY A FEW DAYS AFTER THE MURDER.

HEY.

HMPH.

WHAT WAS THA ABOUT
NOTHING.

SORRY ABOUT THOSE GUYS.
WHISTLE!
FAP FAP FAP FAP
PANT PANT

DOES HE JUST GET OVER THINGS QUICKLY?

WHEN HE SAVED ME FROM SHIMADA HIDEO AS WELL...

SO CALM AND STRONG...
LIKE SOME-ONE ELSE.

UNBELIEVABLY STRONG.

BUT...
WITH KANA, WAS HE REALLY NOT...

NO, THAT'S NOT RIGHT.

EVEN IF THERE WAS NOTHING BETWEEN THEM...

HE'S A LITTLE TOO DISTANT.
GET OUT OF HERE!

RIGHT.
OKAY.

MMM

SORRY, I JUST REMEMBERED SOMETHING.

THE SCHOOL HE GOES TO...

IN THE FALL OF HIS FIRST YEAR, AND THE SUMMER OF HIS SECOND YEAR... TWICE IN ONE YEAR... VIOLENCE BROKE OUT, ON A SCALE NOT SEEN ANY-WHERE ELSE.

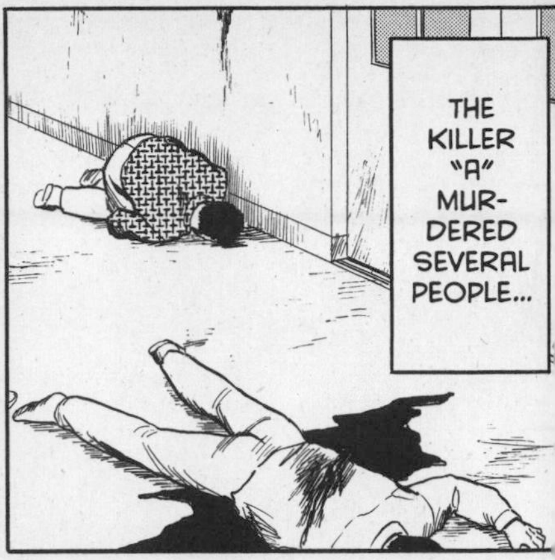
THE KILLER "A" MURDERED SEVERAL PEOPLE...

BEFORE MYSTERIOUSLY EXPLODING.

THEN THE CASE OF SHIMADA HIDEO, THAT SHOCKED THE COUNTRY...

BECAUSE SHIMADA HIDEO—NOT THAT I BELIEVE THIS, MIND—WAS SUPPOSEDLY NOT HUMAN.
AND SEVERAL WITNESSES REPORTED SEEING SHIMADA HIDEO AND IZUMI SHINICHI TALKING.

SHE SEEMS A LITTLE DISTANT, THESE DAYS...

SHE'S UPSET ABOUT KANA, ISN'T SHE?

......

RIGHT!

NOT BEING UPSET IS REALLY WEIRD!

WHICH MEANS I'M WEIRD.
I SHOULDN'T BE SO CALM ABOUT IT.

TALKING TO YOUR-SELF?

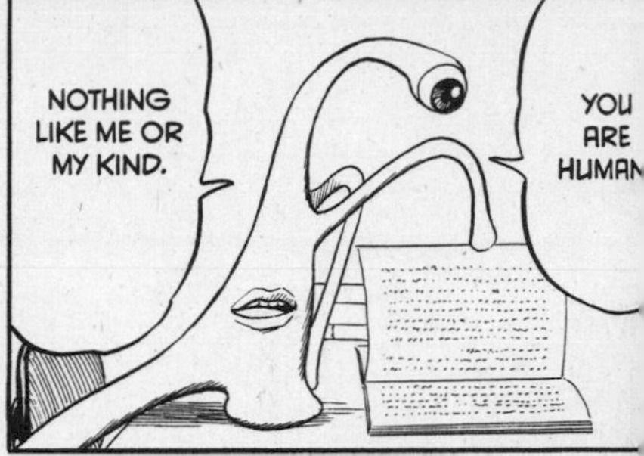
YOU ARE HUMAN
NOTHING LIKE ME OR MY KIND.

FOR SOME REASON...
YOU SAYING THAT MAKES ME EVEN LESS SURE.

ENOUGH SOUND LEAKS WHEN YOU'RE TALKING TO ME. WE ADD IN TALKING TO YOURSELF...

YOUR FATHER'S GONNA START TO NOTICE.

....

THE NEIGHBORS SEEMED TO THINK THE MARRIAGE WAS HAPPY ENOUGH, AND JUST BEFORE SHE VANISHED, THEY WENT ON VACATION TOGETHER.

HIS MOTHER'S DISAP-PEARANCE...

IGNORING GREETINGS FROM FRIENDLY EIGHBORS...

BUT A FEW DAYS LATER SHE CAME BACK ALONE, WITH-OUT ANY LUGGAGE.

SHE WENT INSIDE...

BUT CAME OUT A FEW MINUTES LATER.
......
AND NO ONE'S SEEN HER SINCE.

カタ
TAP
カタ
TAP
カタ
TAP

WELL... DON'T BE TOO LATE.

SURE.

MMM? IT'S AWFULLY LATE...

WHERE'S HE GOING?

KA-
CHUNK
KA-
CHUNK

TWO
STATIONS
AWAY...THIS
TOWN IS...

THE
MURDER
OF THAT
HIGH
SCHOOL
GIRL.
A LOT OF
STRANGE
STUFF
THERE AS
WELL...

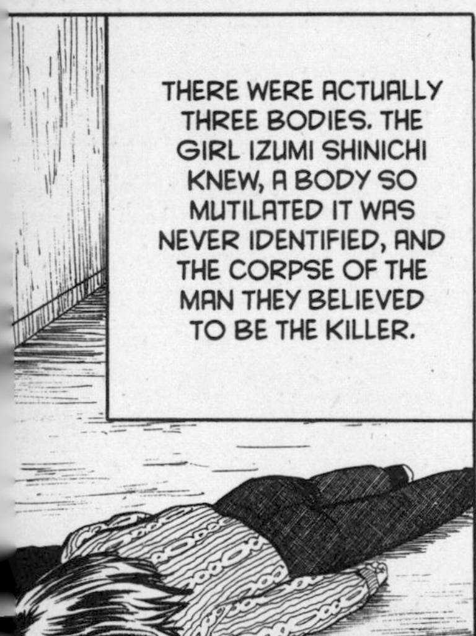
THERE WERE ACTUALLY
THREE BODIES. THE
GIRL IZUMI SHINICHI
KNEW, A BODY SO
MUTILATED IT WAS
NEVER IDENTIFIED, AND
THE CORPSE OF THE
MAN THEY BELIEVED
TO BE THE KILLER.

WHILE THEY WERE CARVING UP THE FIRST BODY, THE HIGH SCHOOL GIRL APPEARED, AND WAS KILLED.

ACCORD-ING TO THE POLICE REPORT, THERE WERE AT LEAST TWO KILLERS...

AT WHICH POINT THE BOY...

THEN THE KILLERS STARTED ARGUING, AND ONE KILLED THE OTHER BEFORE FLEEING THE SCENE.

...IZUMI SHINICHI FOUND THE BODIES.

BUT THEY HAVE SAID NOTHING ABOUT THE IDENTITY OF THE MURDERED KILLER. ARE THERE NO CLUES?

SOMETHING'S GOING ON HERE. IT DOESN'T TAKE A DETECTIVE TO START WONDERING ABOUT A CASE LIKE THIS—IT'S RIGHT OUT OF A MYSTERY NOVEL.

GIVEN THE SHEER NUMBER OF TERRIFYING CASES CROPPING UP AROUND THIS BOY...
HOW CAN I POSSIBLY CALL HIM ORDINARY?

THERE MUST BE SOME-THING...

HE MUST BE HIDING SOME-THING!

IT'S HARD TO BELIEVE, BUT NOW HE'S RETURNING TO THE SCENE OF THE CRIME. TRUTH IS STRANGER THAN FICTION. I THOUGHT HOLMES AND AKECHI KOGORO WERE THE STUFF OF FICTION, BUT...

SHINICHI, WHAT ARE YOU DOING HERE?

IT'S HARD TO EXPLAIN, BUT...
I FEEL LIKE I'M FORGETTING HOW TO FEEL PAIN, OR GRIEF.

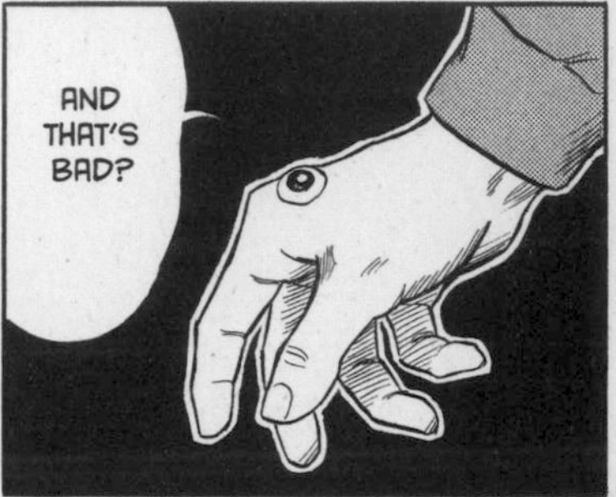
AND THAT'S BAD?

I WASN'T ALWAYS LIKE THIS.
I USED TO OBSESS OVER NOTHING...

I WORRIED FOR DAYS...

Shinichi
Ka

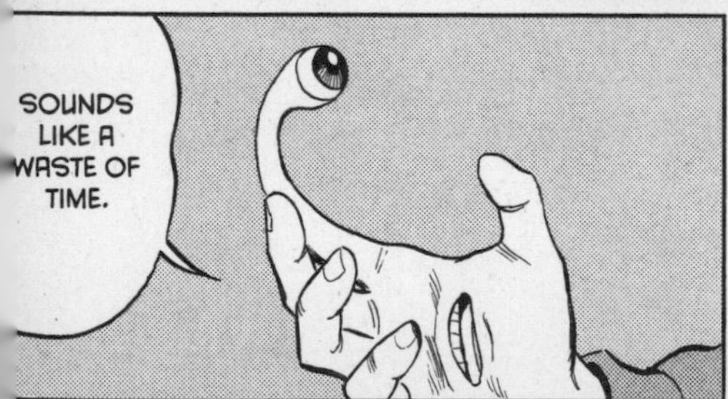
SOUNDS LIKE A WASTE OF TIME.

NOT TRUE!

?

WHO'S HE TALKING TO? HIMSELF?

KANA MUST HAVE THOUGH THAT MONSTE WAS ME.
THAT'S WHY SHE DIED.

IT'S MY FAULT.

THIS IS FOR HER.

YOU SHOULDN'T BLAME YOURSELF.

THIS SOUNDS WEIRD, BUT I WANT TO FEEL SAD THAT SHE DIED.
I DON'T WANT TO FORGET THAT GRIEF.

AS A HUMAN BEING.

HMM...

RUMMAGE

!

ビクッ
TWITCH

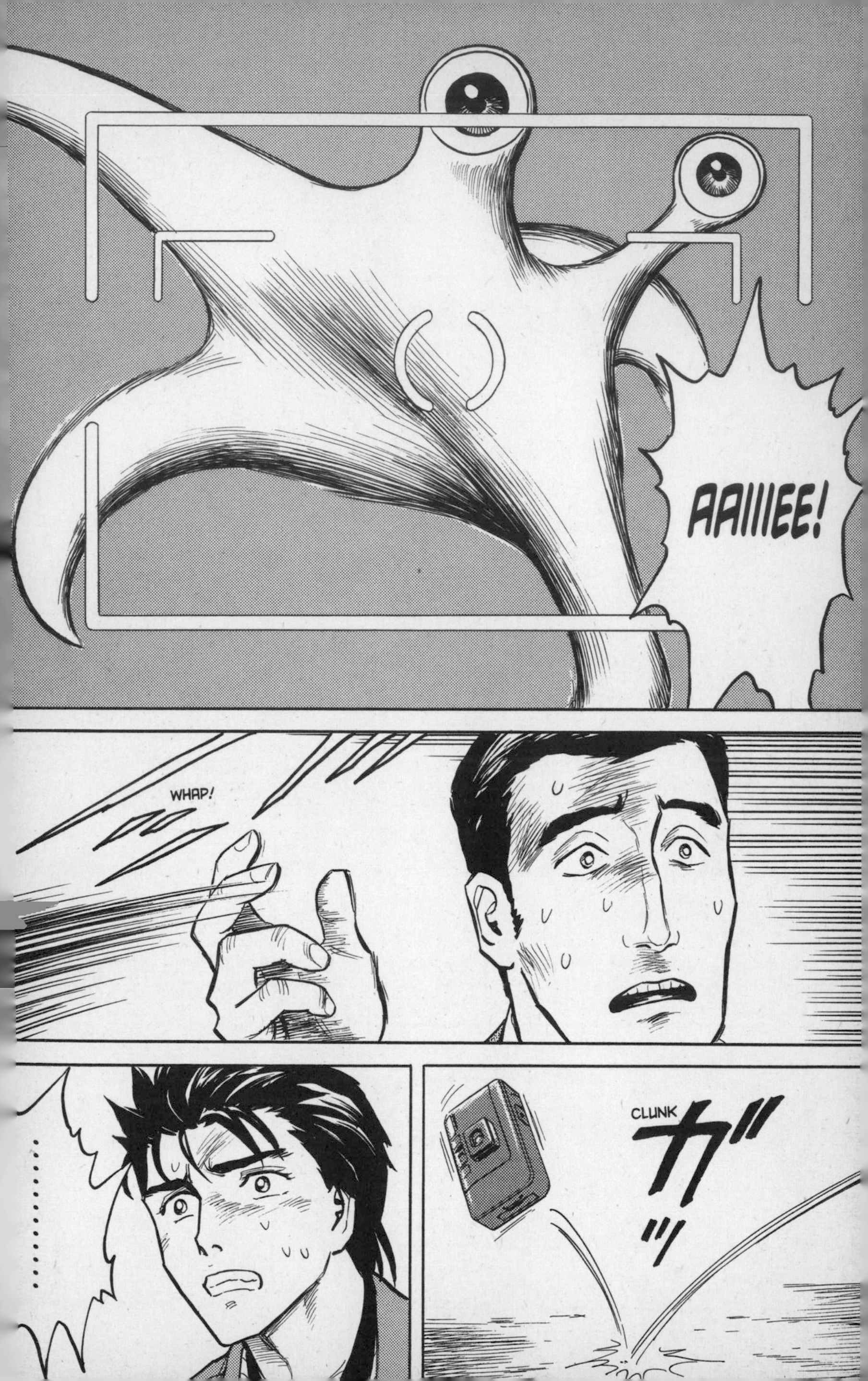
AAIIIIEE!
WHAP!
CLUNK
ガ
ッ

M-
MONSTER!!

ギィィーン

SCHIIING

WAIT, MIGI! WHAT ARE YOU DOING?

WHAT ELSE? KILLING HIM!

NO, WAIT! STOP!

EEEEK!

グイッ
YANK
I SAID, WAIT!

ガッ
CHNK

AAH!
AAAAH!

GET OUT OF HERE! RUN!
NOW!!

WHAT ARE YOU DOING!? RUN!

AAA AHHH...!

DASH

DON'T TRY TO STOP ME SHINICHI.

ギュウウン
WWWWWRRRRR

AAAH!

ヴィン
WWWRRR
AUGH!

OW
ザズ
DRAG

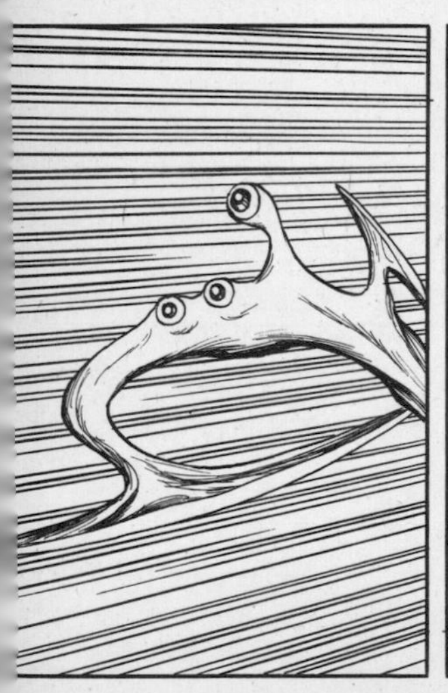

AUGH!
SNIKT

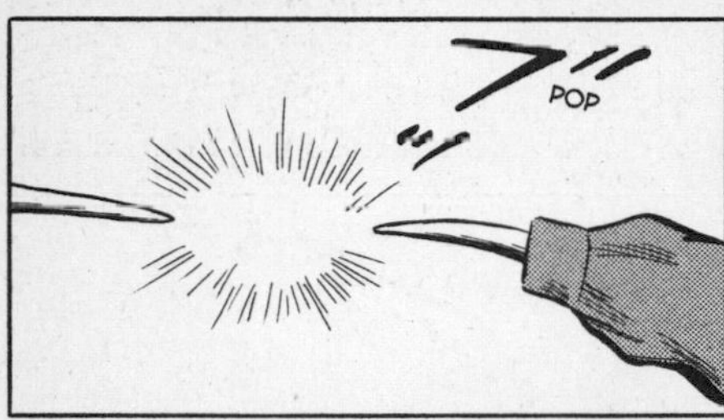
POP

AH!

RUSTLE
YAAH
HAHH

HAHH
HAHH

RUSTLE

RUSTLE

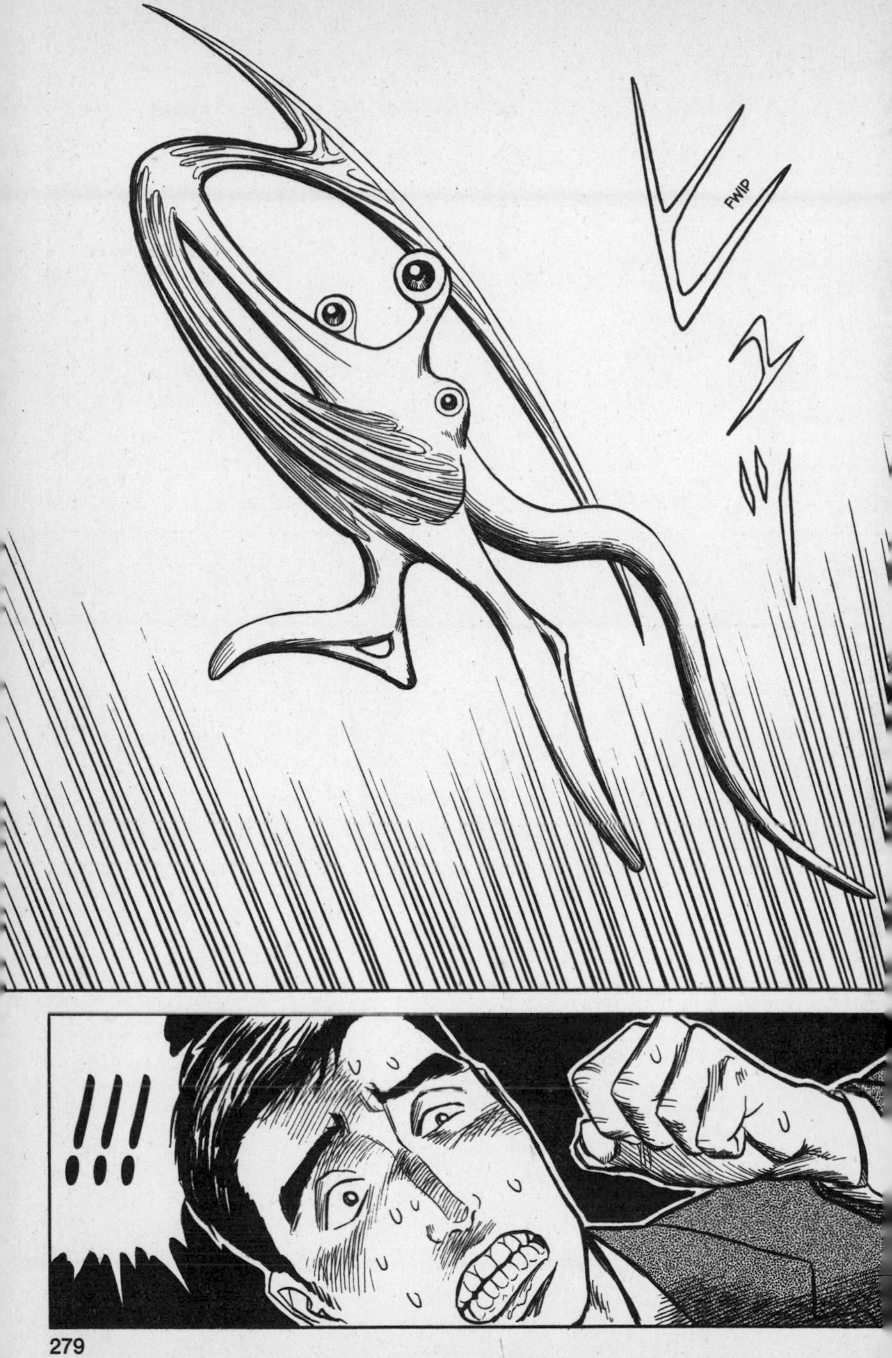

FWIP

CLANG
ガ"
CLANG
ガ"
ARGH!
ビ"
SQRT
ガ"
CLANG

THE BODY'S TOO LIGHT... CAN'T CUT THROUGH...

EEEEK

DAMN!
CAN'T STAY
DISCONNECTED
ANY LONGER...

RUSTLE
RUSTLE

MIGI.....
......

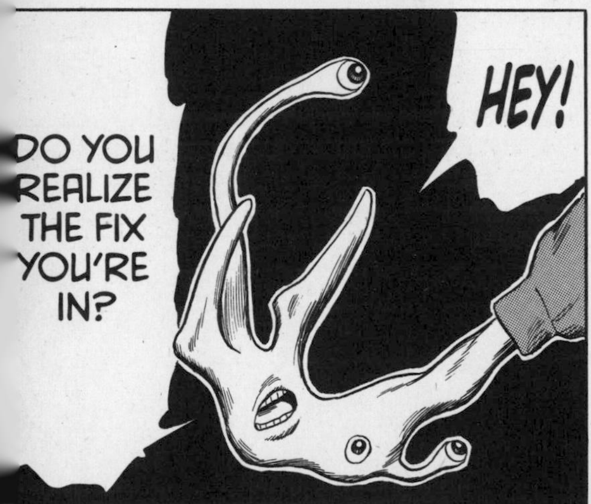
HEY!
DO YOU
REALIZE
THE FIX
YOU'RE
IN?

SPLOOP

WE'VE BEEN SEEN BY SOME STRANGER! WITH A CAMERA!
HE MIGHT KNOW WHO YOU ARE!

CRACK!

S-SEEN...

PARASYTE 4: THE END

TRANSLATION NOTES

Japanese is a tricky language for most Westerners, and translation is often more an art than a science. For your edification and reading pleasure, here are notes on some of the places where we could have gone in a different direction or where a Japanese cultural reference is used.

Maneuvers, page 39

The original word, *enshu*, can be translated as exercise, maneuver, or drill in the military sense.

***Yakuza*, page 43**

Yakuza are, of course, the Japanese mafia.

Heroes, page 74

Iwaaki is making a play on words here. The Japanese word for "hero," as many badly translated robot shows will tell you, means "brave man."

Power, page 139

"Power" here refers to Kana's psychic powers not physical strength.

"Like the wind," page 248

The original Japanese idiom he cites is literally "like a monkey."

Akechi Kogoro, page 265

A detective created by Japan's first mystery writer, Edogawa Rampo. Like Sherlock Holmes, he was extremely intelligent and always outwitted his opponents.

Preview of volume 5 of PARASYTE

We're pleased to present you with a preview from volume 5. Please check our website (www.delreymanga.com) to see when this volume will be available in English. For now you'll have to make do with Japanese!

ガッ

きみは
せいぜい動いて
相手の攻撃を
よけてればいい
いつかみたいに
素手で倒そうなんて
考えるなよ
それで
勝てるのか!?

おっ

ギッ
とっ

ヒョッ

いいぞ なかなかいい 動きだ
これなら 馬の差で勝つな
だれが 馬だって?

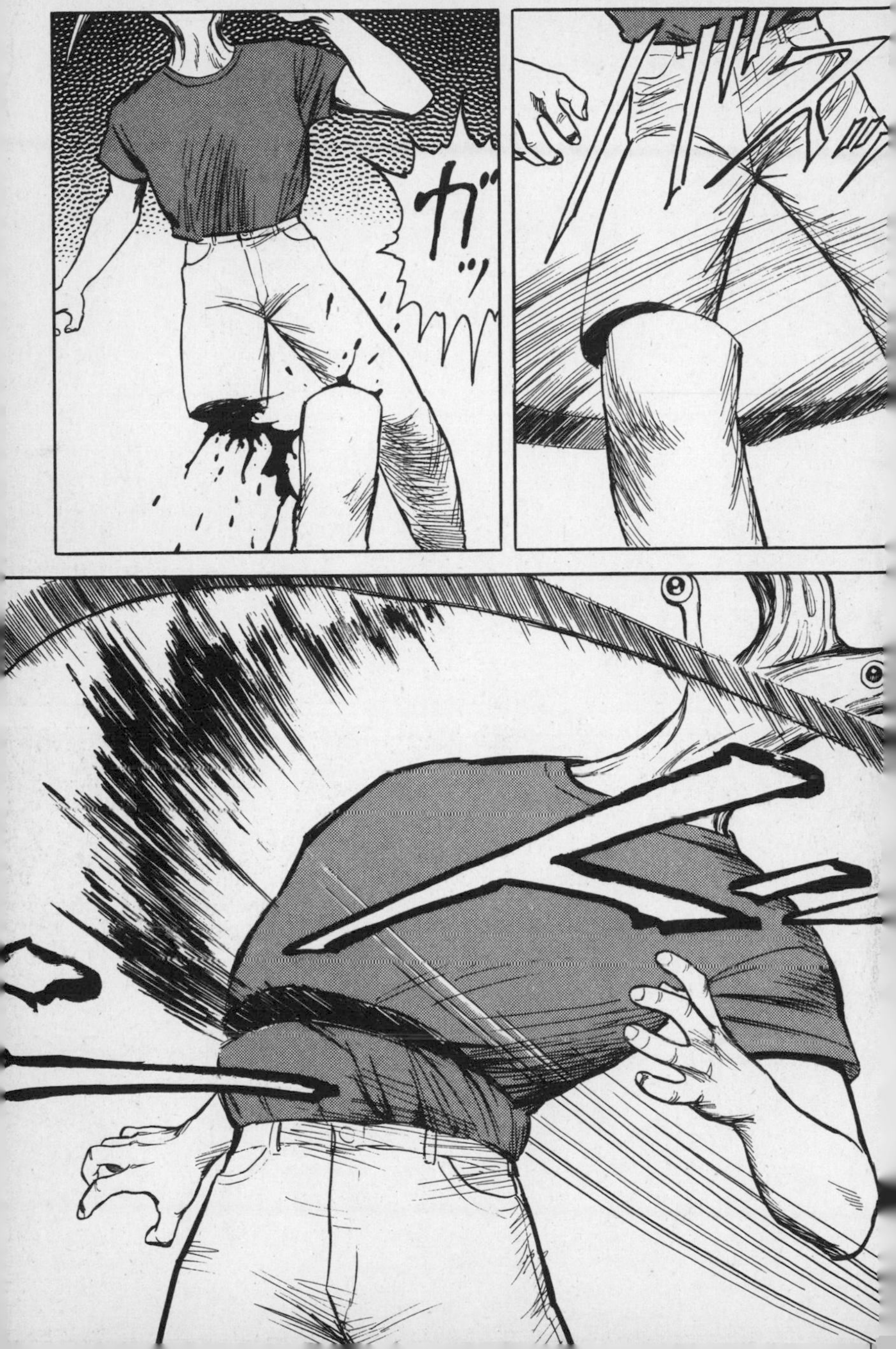

ガッ

やった!!

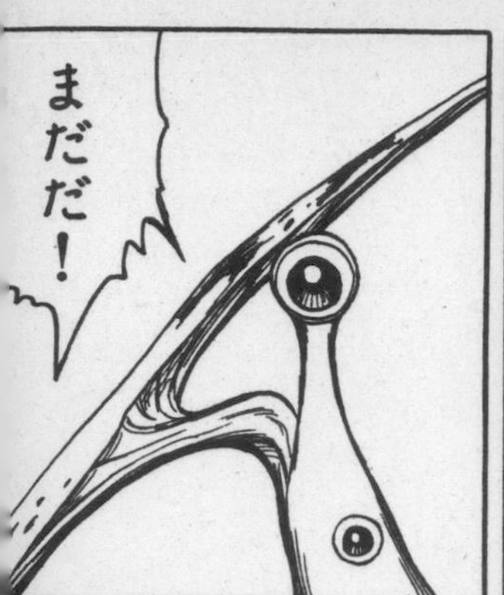
まだだ!

バッ

グブッ

ああああ……………

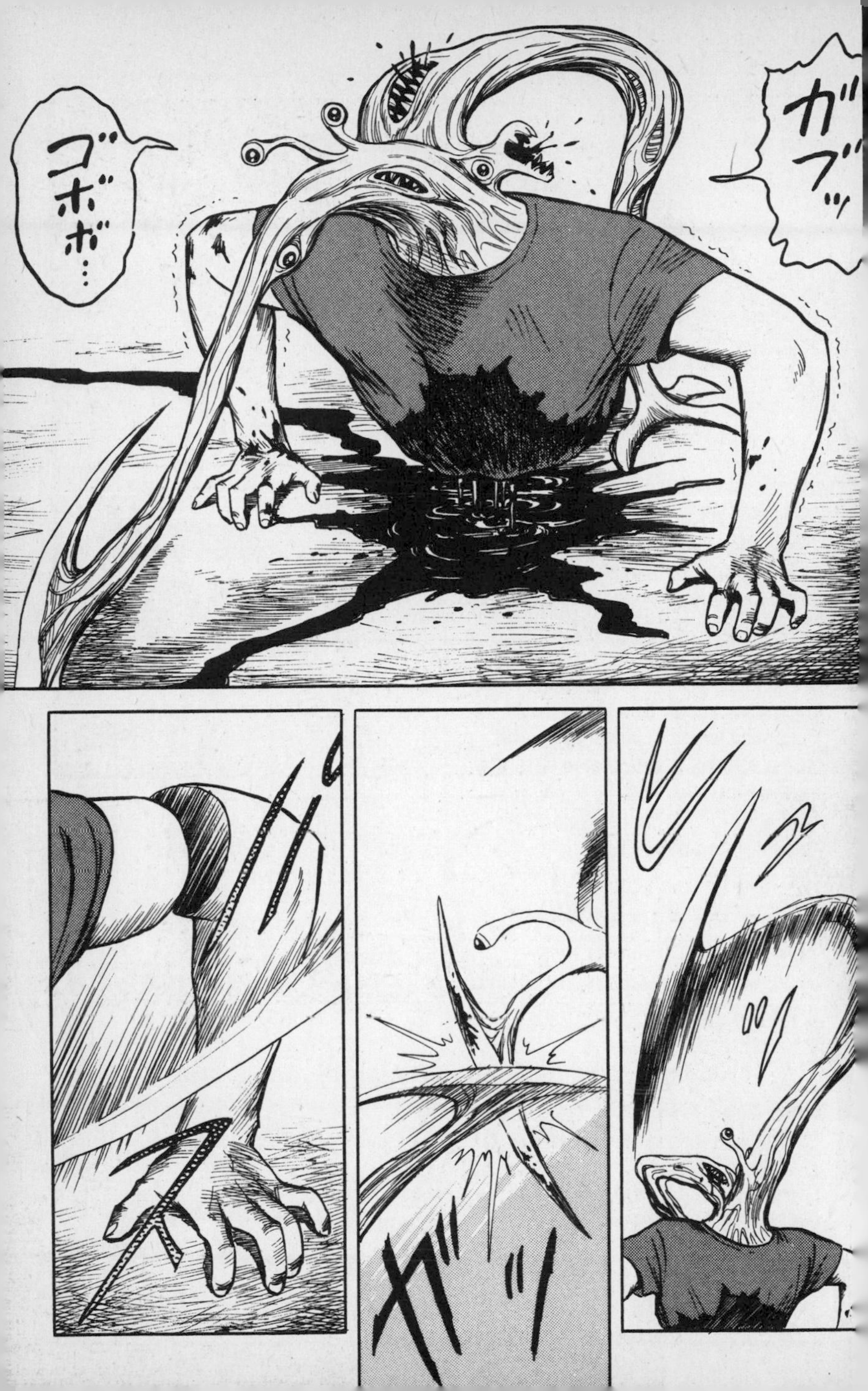

ガブッ

ゴボボ…

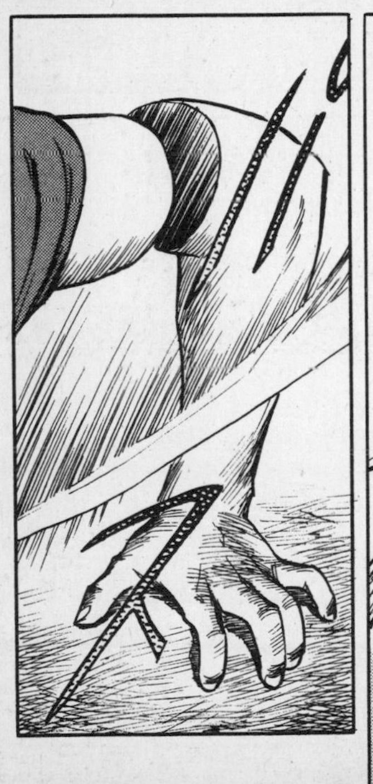

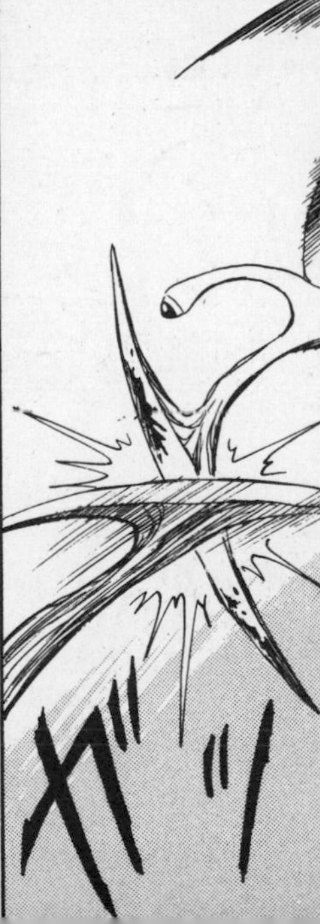

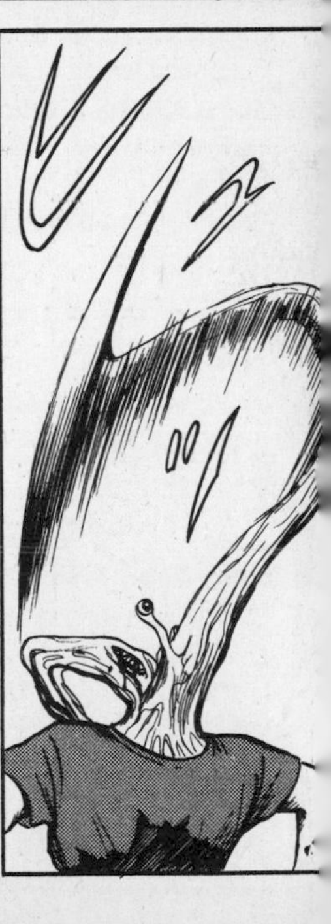

Le Chevalier d'Eon

STORY BY TOU UBUKATA
MANGA BY KIRIKO YUMEJI

DARKNESS FALLS ON PARIS

A mysterious cult is sacrificing beautiful young women to a demonic force that threatens the entire country. Only one man can save Paris from chaos and terror, the king's top secret agent: The Chevalier d'Eon.

- **Available on DVD from ADV Films.**

Special extras in each volume! Read them all!

VISIT WWW.DELREYMANGA.COM TO:
- Read sample pages
- View release date calendars for upcoming volumes
- Sign up for Del Rey's free manga e-newsletter
- Find out the latest about new Del Rey Manga series

RATING OT AGES 16+